Seeking a Center

A portrait of Otto A. Bird, painted by Robert A. Leader, Notre Dame, 1964-65.

OTTO A. BIRD

Seeking a Center

My Life as a Great Bookie

A WETHERSFIELD BOOK
IGNATIUS PRESS   SAN FRANCISCO

Cover design by Marcia Ryan

© 1991 Ignatius Press, San Francisco
All rights reserved
ISBN 0–89870–370–0
Library of Congress catalogue number 91–71555
Printed in the United States of America

*To Mortimer J. Adler,
teacher, friend,
and benefactor*

Things fall apart: the centre cannot hold;
Mere anarchy is loosed upon the world.
—W. B. Yeats

No me poseo sino aqui, en tu abismo,
que envolvidendome todo, eres mi centro,
pues eres Tú más yo que soy yo mismo.
—José de Sigüenza

W. B. Yeats, "The Second Coming", in *The Collected Poems* (New York: Macmillan, 1934), 215.

José de Sigüenza, *Historia de la Orden de San Jerónimo,* quoted by Miguel de Unumono in *Andanzas y visiones españoles* (Madrid: 1959), 14, which translated reads:

> I cannot hold except here in your abyss,
> since encircling me entirely You are my center,
> since You are more I than I am myself.

Contents

Preface by Ralph McInerny	9
I Beginning in Ann Arbor	13
On Becoming a Catholic	14
A Mediaevalist	20
The Theory of Love	22
Great Books	29
Ann Arbor	31
II Pursuing Aristotle in Chicago	35
The Hutchins-Adler Reform	37
Studying Philosophy	40
Catholic Excitement	43
A Contemporary Assessment	44
III Finding the Middles Ages in Toronto	51
The Institute of Mediaeval Studies	52
Graduate Study	55
A Dissertation on Cavalcanti	59
The "Aeterni Patris"	64
Saint Thomas Aquinas	66
IV Becoming a Great Bookie at Notre Dame	73
Founding a Great Books Program	76
Notre Dame's General Program	87
The Program, 1952–63	93
V Making Sense of Philosophy	99
Gilson's Way	101

Adler's Way	106
The Idea of Justice: An Example	110
A Dialectical Solution	115
Two Ways: Gilson's and Adler's	117
VI Recognizing and Holding onto the Center	123
A Work of Recovery	125
Finding a Center	129
Curriculum Vitae	133
Publications by Otto Allen Bird	135
Index of Persons	141

Preface

In Robert Bolt's play *A Man for All Seasons,* when Richard Rich recoils from the suggestion that he become a schoolteacher because whatever he did in that role would be unknown to men, Thomas More replies, "But you would know, your students would know, and God would know." Otto Bird has devoted his life to teaching and, though he would doubtless have been more than content with the obscurity feared by Rich, word of this has gotten out. Not only do his students and colleagues know of it, the wider world has benefited from his choice of vocation. (It goes without saying that God has been privy to Otto's doings.)

It has been said of Gilbert Keith Chesterton's *Autobiography* that it is about everyone except Chesterton. No more does Otto Bird's book fall into the confessional genre of autobiography. He calls it an intellectual autobiography; it narrates the journey of an intellect, of a soul, and puts before the reader a vision of the intellectual life one wishes were more palpably present in Catholic colleges and universities than it nowadays is. In the title of a talk by his mentor Etienne Gilson, Otto's life has been a story of "The Intellect in the Service of Christ the King".

There is at present much talk of the nature of the Catholic university. It is asked whether a university can be at once great and Catholic, an astonishing question given the provenance of the modern university. Often it is suggested that if the Mass is said on campus and students are sensitive to the material needs of the less fortunate, a university deserves to be called Catholic. Otto Bird reminds us of a better time, when it was understood that the faith should animate imagination and mind as well as the corporal works of mercy. Indeed, what is peculiar to the Catholic university is precisely that in its halls intellectual and imaginative pursuits are seen in terms of the great journey mankind is on toward salvation. It is curiously true that the fact that this life is a mere prelude to the true life men are meant for hereafter, far from devaluing the things of this world, enhances them and casts over them a light they could not have otherwise. "Love calls us to the things of this world", Richard Wilbur wrote, and the line stands even when the love involved is the theological virtue. Faith and Hope and Love do not make one disdainful of this world but rather, by seeing it as the stage on which one's eternal condition will be settled, give it far profounder significance than it could have if "our little lives were rounded in a sleep". The evanescent things about us, the fleeting things whose season swiftly comes and goes, nonetheless are messages from One who never changes, a scattering of Sybil's leaves from which we can read, however obscurely, intimations of God. The reader will find in the pages that follow an exuberant romance with the world on the part of one whose destination is heaven.

It has been my privilege to know Otto Bird as a colleague for some thirty-six years. Slowly and over time one comes to see that some of one's colleagues, seemingly ordinary folk encountered day by day, engaged in the common task, are extraordinary persons, truly great. It is clear to me as it is to many others that Otto Bird is one of the great professors of the University of Notre Dame. His influence on students and colleagues is at once incalculable and inescapable. His work beyond the campus with Mortimer Adler has extended his reach to thousands upon thousands of others. I am delighted that his book is published under the aegis of the Wethersfield Institute, as the first in a series to be published with Ignatius Press. May this little book touch the minds and hearts of many and stand as a reminder of a magnificent man who understood his vocation clearly and lived it to the full.

Ralph McInerny

Chapter One

Beginning in Ann Arbor

Life in this world began for me in Ann Arbor, Michigan, on July 3, 1914, or so I have been told. For most of my childhood I lived in Ann Arbor in the vicinity of the old central campus of the University of Michigan. The Ann Arbor Press, which my uncle owned and operated, did much work for the university, since in those days it had no press of its own. Thus I grew up equating Ann Arbor with its university. However, this beginning of mine is not the one that I am here and now concerned with, except incidentally.

The beginning that I would recapture now through memory and recollection is the one that made me into a Roman Catholic in religion, a mediaevalist in scholarship, and a reader, teacher, and advocate of great books by profession. The development that had these three results had its beginning in Ann Arbor—a beginning that led me from there to Chicago, then on to Toronto, and eventually to Notre Dame.

I can see now many years later to what extent those beginnings have reached or are approaching an end. I became a Catholic, and, in continuing to believe and practice that religion, I am still at a beginning and will not know until death whether I have reached the hoped-for end that it promises.

I did become a mediaevalist and made a few contributions to the study and understanding of mediaeval thought, but it is unlikely that I will make any more, although my interest in the Middle Ages still remains.

Great books I still read; I established a college program based upon reading them, which still exists at Notre Dame, and, although I seldom engage in teaching them any longer, I do continue to write occasionally about them.

On Becoming a Catholic

The first of the beginnings that I have mentioned is also the most difficult one to write about. Unless one is a Saint Augustine, to provide an account of a religious conversion is especially difficult, since at root it is based on the mystery of the workings of divine grace.

Yet the circumstances surrounding that move for me were clear and definite. I was admitted into the Catholic Church in September 1932, at the start of my second year at the University of Michigan. Until that time in my eighteenth year I had not known well any Catholics with the single exception of an American-Irish woman thirty years of age, whom I had met the previous year at the house of a friend. During my high school years on the Mexican border in Nogales, Arizona, I had known many Catholics, since they composed a majority of my fellow students, but I knew none of them well and never discussed matters of religion with any of them. With my Grandmother Bird I regularly attended the Episcopalian church of Saint Andrew's and became well acquainted with its young rector, and my grandmother

Beginning in Ann Arbor

may have held some hope that I would become a priest. I still wear the silver cross that she gave me when I entered the university. Following my father's example, I had become an avid reader of the works of G. K. Chesterton, including even the more apologetic writings.

While attending the university during my first year in Ann Arbor, I continued to attend the Episcopalian church. It had a much larger congregation than I had been used to, and one that was also much more diverse. It contained members who considered themselves to belong variously either to a low, a middle, or a high church, each group feeling itself free to believe and practice as it thought best. Apart from the individual person, it appeared that there was no authority over either belief or practice. I found such diversity and difference confusing and unsettling. The rector in my Arizona church had provided me with a letter of introduction to the priest in Ann Arbor, and he was kind in directing me to activities that I would enjoy. Thus if a high Episcopalian priest were officiating, I would usually be asked to serve as his altar boy. That was satisfying up to a point, for it indicated that I was thought to believe in the Real Presence of Our Lord at the altar, and so I did; but I also knew that there were few in the entire congregation who shared in that belief.

My dissatisfaction and disaffection were such that I accepted an invitation from a Christian student association to attend a meeting of one of their groups known as the Upper Room. But from the very opening of the meeting I recognized that their way was not for me. It began with a song, a kind of hymn, celebrating the belief that having no creed makes one free. That position was not one for me, even if at that time I was unfortunately in it; I certainly had no desire to remain in a state of non-credal disbelief. The Episcopalian church was bad enough in this respect, but the Upper Room was worse. What I was seeking was not the lack and absence of a creed, but the presence of a strong and definite one, so that one might locate himself with some confidence not only in this world but also in the world to come.

From this account of my memory of my situation then, I must have been looking for more from religious faith than I had been able to find so far. But why should I have looked to the Catholic Church as a source that could satisfy that need?

I came to the decision to do so during the summer vacation after my first year at the university. The first part of that summer I spent with cousins on Bois Blanc Island in the north end of Lake Huron. For reading I took with me two books: the *Don Quixote* of Cervantes and the compilation *Irish Fairy and Folk Tales,* edited by W. B. Yeats. Both works portray a world filled with the beliefs and practices of Catholicism. Both are also mainly concerned with the contrast between the phenomenal world of practical experience and the ideal world of imagination and belief. Moved by that reading, I came to the conclusion that I had to find a belief according to which I could live, and act, and think. And I suspected strongly that that belief was to be found in the Roman Catholic Church.

Although inclined both by affection and by imagination toward that belief, I was still ignorant of much of its teaching. To remedy that defect, I turned to Cardinal Newman's account of his conversion in the *Apologia pro vita sua*.¹ My situation was a little comparable to his in that I too was an Episcopalian or Anglican Christian in the process of considering becoming a Roman Catholic. Another similarity, I soon discovered, was the mistrust that Newman had as a youth that material phenomena exhaust the nature of reality. For a time, he wrote, he "used to wish that the Arabian Tales were true", and even wondered whether "all this world was a deception, my fellow-angels, by a playful device concealing themselves from me, and deceiving me with the semblance of a natural world".² The answer to his doubt he found in the sacramental principle that holds that "the exterior world, physical and historical, [is] but the outward manifestation of realities greater than itself".³ A preeminent instance of the principle is the sacrament of the Holy Eucharist, where the hidden reality is radically different from and greater than the phenomena under which it appears.

The other doctrines of faith that Newman claimed were of major importance in his search I was also well prepared to accept. The first of these, which he called the "principle of dogma", maintains that the Christian faith is more than a demand of emotion and sentiment in that it also proclaims truths about the way things are. "The drama of religion and the combat of truth and error", he wrote, "are ever one and the same".⁴ The beliefs originating in the revelation of God as well

---

[1] J. H. Newman, *Apologia pro vita sua* (London: J. M. Dent, Everyman Library, 1921).
[2] Ibid., 29.
[3] Ibid., 49.
[4] Ibid., 67.

as the understanding of them both fall within the realm of the unity of truth.

Another doctrine based on the truth of dogma is that there exists "a visible church with sacraments and rites which are the channels of invisible grace",[5] and that this church is the Roman Catholic Church.

The other basic principle underlying Newman's conversion follows from the claim made for truth. It lies in the demand for a resolution of "the conflict between reason and affection".[6] Since truths are to be grasped and understood, which is the work of reason, affection alone without reason cannot provide a sound and solid basis for the acceptance of the Catholic faith.

By the end of the summer of 1932 I felt confident that I could and would make my own the preceding principles. I therefore went to consult the chaplain of Saint Mary's Chapel at the University of Michigan and after a period of instruction was received into the Roman Catholic Church.

Recollecting now those books that I read almost sixty years ago, reconsidering their effect upon me at that time, I do not think it an exaggeration to claim that *Don Quixote* was the most influential. In ways that seem puzzling and obscure, that book persuaded me that I too should become a Catholic and to that extent at least follow that great knight of faith.

It may seem odd that Don Quixote, who is often taken as no more than a figure of fun and of ridicule, should ever inspire anyone to become a Catholic. Given this oddity, it may be worth considering why it is a possibility. For this purpose I draw upon an essay that

[5] Ibid., 119.
[6] Ibid., 71.

I wrote more than fifty years later that develops a thesis put forward by the English poet, W. H. Auden, that Don Quixote is the portrait of a Christian saint presented under the guise of irony.[7]

The ironic hero differs from all other heroes of literature—whether epic, tragic, or comic—in not being at all what he seems. However it may appear to others, however ridiculous even as a parody of the ideal that he seeks to achieve, Don Quixote acts according to the faith that inspires his ideal and undergoes all the suffering that action entails without either complaint or despair. His virtues, which are many, flow from that faith and not from pride. That faith and the strength of the conviction with which it is held separate Don Quixote from his followers, even from his Sancho, and much more, of course, from those who share none of his belief. His love of chivalry is a trait that he shares with such saints as Saint Teresa and Saint Ignatius Loyola, as is his endeavor to revive and restore an ideal that has been neglected and impoverished even when not entirely lost. In fact, he dares to equate the profession that he has taken up with the peace proclaimed in the Gospel:

> The first good news the world and mankind received was that which the angels announced on the night that was our day, when they sang in the air, "Glory to God in the highest, and peace on earth to men of good will"; and the salutation which the great Master of heaven and earth taught his disciples and chosen followers when they

---

[7] "The Ambiguities of Don Quixote", in *The Great Ideas Today*, 1984 (Chicago: Encyclopaedia Britannica, 1984), 95–122. The Auden essay, entitled "The Ironic Hero", appeared in *Horizon Magazine* 20 (1949): 86–93.

entered any house, was to say, "Peace be on this house"; and many other times he said to them, "My peace I give unto you, my peace I leave you, peace be with you"; a jewel and a precious gift given and left by such a hand: a jewel without which there can be no happiness either on earth or in heaven [D. Q. I. chap. 37].[8]

Don Quixote in his history proclaims himself in word and deed as a knight of belief, and the way in which he confirms it applies equally well to the Christian faith. The first is that things do not always seem or appear the same to everybody: they appear one way to the believer and another way to the non-believer. The second is that desire is an important element in belief. Don Quixote, in fact, provides an apt although ironic illustration of the claim that William James put forward in his essay, "The Will to Believe".[9] There James argues that in matters of belief the passional or non-intellectual side of our nature provides an essential ingredient that is especially influential in matters where there is an option to which neither reason nor sense experience of themselves can determine an answer. For James and Don Quixote, as for Pascal, "the heart has reasons that reason cannot fathom".

A Mediaevalist

Upon entering the university I was even more ignorant of the Christian Middle Ages than I was of Catholicism.

---

[8] *Don Quixote* has been quoted according to the translation of John Ormsby, in *Great Books of the Western World* (Chicago: Encyclopaedia Britannica, year), 29:145d–46a.

[9] William James, *The Will to Believe and Other Essays in Popular Philosophy* (New York: Longman's, Green, and Co., 1915), 1–31.

Almost all that I knew about it came from what Chesterton had written in praise of it. However, during the first semester of classes there several things happened that attracted my interest to that period. During the high school years my strongest bent had been toward mathematics and physics. Detecting that interest, my father, who was a lawyer, to lead me away from the pursuit of an academic career, persuaded me to direct my interest in science to the study of medicine. Accordingly, as a freshman I enrolled in the "Pre-Med Program". This program in 1931 at Ann Arbor required a knowledge of Latin, which I lacked, as well as a continuation of the study of chemistry. The latter requirement serves as something of a test of a student's seriousness in the pursuit of a medical career. One semester of chemistry sufficed to indicate that I failed that test. Latin had the opposite effect. I much enjoyed it, although I was not particularly good at it, and for several semesters I pursued courses in the Latin department. My attachment grew stronger after I became a Catholic and learned to pray in Latin.

The required course in history during the first semester studied the period in Europe from the fall of Rome to 1648 and thus devoted much attention to the Middle Ages; it so awakened my interest in that period that I followed three more courses on mediaeval history and civilization.

I also soon began the study of mediaeval literature. At first this amounted to courses in Anglo-Saxon, Chaucer, and mediaeval literature, all offered by the English department. It was not until I entered upon graduate work that I began to study other mediaeval languages. The master's degree that I obtained was in effect in comparative literature. Since there was no such department in Ann Arbor in 1935–36, the English department offered me a base, with the help of Professor John Reinhard, the principal mediaevalist there at the time.

I followed a year-long course in Dante in Italian, after having devoted a summer to learning the language. With Reinhard, I followed his year-long course in Chaucer in Middle English. The same professor accepted me, as his only seminar student, for the study of the mediaeval lyric in Provençal, Italian, French, and English. He helped me draw up a series of readings that I had to study and then discuss with him once a week. This we did throughout the academic year with but two exceptions. Once I asked to be excused to attend the funeral of my maternal grandmother; the other occurred when on arriving at his office I found him talking to a beautiful woman, not at all a university type, and he excused himself from that day's discussion with me. He helped me to prepare as my master's thesis a short study of the role of literary convention in the mediaeval love lyric. For the Italian course I wrote on Dante's theory of love. While writing about love, I was also suffering under its passion, so much so that within a year I was married.

The Theory of Love

Love, at least in the writings about it, continued to provide me with a subject of study after I left Ann Arbor. It supplied me with the dissertation topic for which I received the doctoral degree in philosophy at the University of Toronto in 1939. Dante's *primo amico,*

Guido Cavalcanti, wrote a famous "Canzone d'Amore", entitled after its beginning "Donna mi priega" ("A lady asks me"). Dino del Garbo, a Florentine physician and natural philosopher, wrote a commentary upon this, and it was this that I edited, translated from its Latin, and annotated with historical and philosophical observations. Del Garbo's commentary was almost contemporary with the poem, since its author died in 1327, just twenty-seven years after the death of Cavalcanti.

The study of love broadened and intensified for me, culminating years later when, in 1961, I joined a team of six engaged in analyzing the major theories of love with the aim of charting and clarifying the controversy on that subject. This research eventually resulted in a large book, entitled *The Idea of Love,* which was written by Robert Hazo and published in 1967. Participating in this research led me to develop a plan of my own for describing and analyzing theories of love, a plan that became the basis for several courses taught at Notre Dame in the early 1970s.

As I saw it then and still maintain, the complexity of love and of the theories about it are best disentangled by the use of two general principles: one is the identification of the kind of love that an author takes as a paradigm for all the basic varieties of love; the other is the number of analytical components that an author employs in the construction of his theory.

Classical Greek had no one word for all the loves such as English possesses in the word "love". Hence, to speak of love in Greek usually amounted to referring to only one kind of love. There were for this purpose four basic words: *eros, philia, storge,* and *agape.* This linguistic fact had both an advantage and a disadvantage. The advantage lay in the fact that talk about love was usually about one definite kind of love: about *eros* or erotic love; *philia* or friendship; *storge* or affection, especially that between parents and children; or *agape,* the regard and affection that one has for a superior. The disadvantage of having no one word such as the English "love" appeared when one attempted to deal with all the four kinds as somehow one, for this effort tended to result in the attempt to make one kind paradigmatic of all the rest.

The clearest example of this tendency is the account of *philia* that Aristotle gives in the *Nicomachean Ethics* (bks. 8–9) as well as in the *Eudemian Ethics*.[10] That he is demanding a lot of work from *philia* is clear from the many uses that he claims can be made of it: it can be said of family members, kinsmen, comrades, children, parents, husbands and wives, the hospitality shown to guests and foreigners, to the erotic relationship, and even to oneself. However, *philia* cannot be had for wine, for the cosmos, or for God, since in these cases Aristotle maintains there can be no reciprocity.

That the main and paradigmatic use of *philia* is for that which we call friendship is clear from his assertion that *philia* is an analogical term. In its range of uses it does not always refer to one and the same thing, or to the species of one genus, and yet it is not entirely equivocal. For all of its uses are related to one that is primary. In this respect *philia* is like the word "surgical", which can be said of an instrument, of a person, or of a certain

---

[10] Aristotle, *Magna Moralia,* 1209a20–35; *Ethica Eudemia* 1236a16–30; *Ethica Nicomacheia,* VIII–IX.

knowledge. It is the last one of these that is primary, since it is the knowledge that is the cause and principle of the instrument being of use in surgery, just as it is the possession of that knowledge that qualifies a person as a surgeon.

To identify the primary reference of *philia,* Aristotle distinguishes three kinds of goods that can serve as its object: those that came to be known in Latin as the *utile,* the *delectabile,* and the *honestum.* Accordingly, there are three corresponding friendships: a friendship for utility, such as the partners in a business venture; one exclusively for pleasure, such as a man seeks in a bordello; and a friendship for that which is intrinsically good, as good in and for itself. This last one provides the primary reference and the paradigm for all the others and is exemplified in the friendship of two good and equal persons who are devoted to the good, and which also has its share of utility and pleasure. The other two friendships are like it but are not as complete, and in fact may not be morally good at all. An erotic relationship may at an extreme seek nothing but pleasure and be neither useful nor morally good, just as a business friendship may also be based on nothing but its utility for those who are associated only for this reason.

In still another respect, Aristotle's analysis of *philia* is exemplary for one wanting to understand theories of love. It avoids the attempt to locate one univocal definition for all the varieties of love. While maintaining that *philia* is primary, he claims that three analytical terms are needed to identify and distinguish the basic kinds of love. These three terms are provided by the three senses of "good" that he distinguishes: the *utile, delectabile,* and *honestum.*

By identifying and disengaging the two general principles that Aristotle uses in his account of *philia,* we can obtain a method for understanding and comparing the various theories of love. A brief illustration of how such a method may be applied is provided in the following.

The first cut that separates theories of love is obtained by identifying the kind of love that is taken as the paradigm for all the rest. In the ancient world of the West it is *philia* or *amicitia* that holds the place of honor, with Aristotle and Cicero its main exponents. In the Christian Middle Ages it is *agape,* the love of charity found in God's love for us and our love for God, that is primary and with reference to which all the other loves can be explained, as in the theologies of Saint Augustine and Saint Thomas Aquinas. It is not until our modern times that the erotic love of man and woman is considered to be the essential one for understanding the nature of love.

The number of analytical terms that a theory employs as the elements or components needed to account for the primary love and its difference from others provides the means for making a second cut among theories of love. Some theories are monadic in that they claim that all love at its root derives from but one element. Thus for Freud all love comes from the energy of libido seeking sexual gratification,[11] whereas for Scheler it derives from a reaction to value and its enhancement.[12] Other theories are dyadic in that they claim two elements are

[11] Sigmund Freud, "Group Psychology and the Analysis of the Ego", in *Great Books of the Western World* (Chicago: Encyclopaedia Britannica), 54:673b–c.

[12] Max Scheler, *The Nature of Sympathy,* trans. Peter Heath, pt. 2 (New Haven, Conn: Yale University Press, 1954), 147–65.

needed to explain the phenomenon of love. Such is the case of D'Arcy in his use of the notions of *animus* and *anima*,[13] and so too of Nygren with his distinction between *eros* as a wholly self-centered love and *agape* as entirely directed toward another person and his good.[14] Triadic theories are those like that of Aristotle that require three basis elements or components.

Of the triadic theories, I find that the most suggestive and convincing is the one that C. S. Lewis proposed in the book entitled *The Four Loves,* which was first published in 1960.[15] As the title indicates, the book was not intended as a systematic and detailed exposition of a triadic theory of love. Rather, he offered that theory as the best way he could find of describing the four loves with which he was concerned, namely, affection, friendship, eros, and charity. The three components he identified as Need-Love, Appreciative-Love, and Gift-Love. These three are capable of a much fuller exploitation than Lewis gave to them, and, as rich as his book is, to do so would make his account still richer. The simplest and briefest way of indicating such a development may be by means of a simple diagram, such as the one on page 28.

Let the three component-loves each be represented by a circle and so arranged as to intersect and form seven regions. The three external regions not intersecting with any other represent each of the components in its pure state, as it were: naked need entirely self-seeking

---

[13] M. C. D'Arcy, *The Mind and Heart of Love* (New York: Meridian Books, 1956).

[14] Anders Nygren, *Agape and Eros,* trans. P. S. Watson (London: S.P.C.K, 1953).

[15] C. S. Lewis, *The Four Loves* (New York: Harcourt, Brace, 1960).

THE DIAGRAM OF LOVE

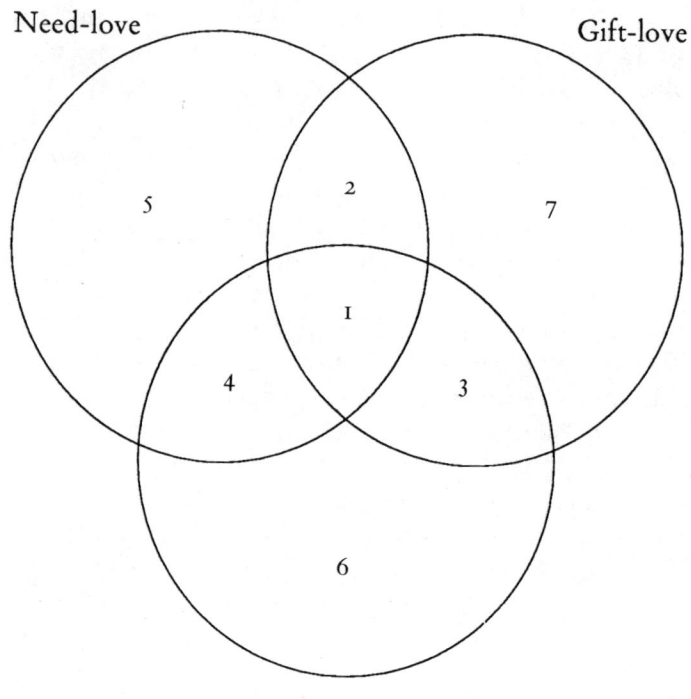

without any mixture of appreciation or benevolence, pure appreciation and admiration regardless of needing or giving, and pure giving-love as in the charity of God.

There are three regions where two of the circles overlap: the union of Need- and Gift-Love as in the affection of a parent for an unworthy and unlovely child; that of Gift- and Appreciative-Love where there is no need of the self apart from the admiring and the giving; and third, the union of Appreciative- and Need-Love, as in the love of knowledge that is a need of the self but which may be directed toward an object for which there is no possibility of giving, such as an astronomer's love for the stars.

Finally, there is one region in which all three circles overlap, which diagrams the union of Need- Gift- Appreciative-Love. As such, it best represents the paradigm of any complex theory of love that has need of at least these three components. So much is true whether the paradigm be friendship as it is for Aristotle, or erotic love as Lewis conceived of it, or the love of charity that God has for us and that we by divine grace have for him.

Great Books

Ann Arbor provided still another beginning for me, although at the time I was not aware of it. The major academic concentration of my undergraduate years came in the second semester of my junior year, when I was chosen as one of the twenty or so students for the English Honors Program. This program demanded almost all of the student's time for three semesters: I recall taking only two courses outside of it. Besides the extensive reading and study that it demanded, there were two meetings to attend. Each student had a major professor as his tutor to whom he reported once a week, often with a written essay. The high point of the week, however, was the discussion seminar in which the class met with a professor to discuss together the book assigned for the week's reading. Up until I entered it, the entire senior year had been devoted to reading very extensively in English literature from Spenser down to the twentieth century. But the year that I was in it, it was world rather than English literature that provided the books for reading and discussion. It thus came to approximate more closely the Great Books seminar that I was to know later on.

By the time I was a senior I had become much interested in poetry, and especially in that of Ezra Pound and T. S. Eliot. The work of both poets was highly suspect to many professors then in the English department. I had been introduced to the work of Pound by a graduate student from the University of Ohio, who had come to Ann Arbor to compete for the prize money awarded each year by the Avery Hopwood writing contest. The prizes came from a large bequest that the dramatist of that name, known best for the horror play and film, *The Bat,* had given to the university in order to encourage creative writing. The prizes in the early 1930s were munificent: $1,500 for a major award, which was then a large sum of money, since tuition amounted to only $50 a semester, and two small rooms could be rented for $30 a month. Such amounts as prizes attracted hopeful young writers from far and wide. The friend just mentioned, himself a protégé of Pound, won a major prize for poetry, and I obtained a minor prize for poetry the following year when Pound was one of the judges.

My interest in Pound and Eliot did not cause me

any particular difficulty until the time of final examinations. In the first place, in writing about Milton, I had adopted the position taken by Eliot that anyone writing poetry in our day would be ruined by following Milton's practice and should on all accounts steer clear of that poet and his influence. This of itself gave me a low standing with the professor of Milton. But with him I fared still worse with the senior essay I wrote on the subject of comedy and satire. He charged that I had intentionally quoted provocative passages from poets and writers that were lewd and obscene. For that I was told that I was in danger of losing an honors degree. However, that eventuality failed to take place, largely, I believe, from the defense offered by my tutor, who had directed my essay, which at his suggestion was based on Meredith's essay on comedy.

Ann Arbor

For me Ann Arbor proved to be fertile in beginnings, although at the time they were happening I was not aware of where they might lead, if anywhere at all. In the 1930s Ann Arbor still remained the small country town that it had long been. There was a sharp division (including a "Division Street") between "Town and Gown", although students did not wear gowns except at the graduation exercises. Banks closed on Wednesdays and remained open on Saturdays for the benefit of the farmers who then came to town. There was a "Farmers and Mechanics" bank. The population was in the twenty thousands, and the town had not yet become more or less a suburb of Detroit, as it now is. The university itself had about ten thousand students in my day; it had three thousand in 1914 when my father attended it and one thousand in 1900 when my Uncle Otto graduated.

When I lived there as a boy and a university student, there were on the east side of town, where the university was located, many handsome old houses in the neighborhood, surrounded by large spaces and silences, among which I lived and played. We were dwelling then, my mother, grandmother, sister, and I, on Maynard Street, across from the Nichols Arcade, which connected Maynard with State Street, and close to the old Majestic Theatre. As young children we could sneak into the latter by mounting the fire-escape stairs into the balcony and watch a movie in which Harold Lloyd, the "human fly", climbed up the side of a building.

Across the street from the Majestic was the Ann Arbor Press, which was owned and operated by my Uncle Otto Hans. He had bought it in the early 1900s and made it in effect into the university press. The student paper, the *Michigan Daily,* was printed on its presses, as well as many of the books written by university professors—all before either the *Daily* or the university had built presses of their own.

My uncle had come to the University of Michigan in 1894 from South Bend, Indiana, and had soon obtained a place for himself on the infant student paper and turned it into a business that was profitable to himself as well as to the paper. It sent him to the 1900 Olympic Games in Paris, and he continued to operate it as a successful business until the regents of the university ruled that he could no longer qualify as a student and hence had to leave the *Daily*. It was then that he obtained

Beginning in Ann Arbor

a printing establishment of his own, which he ran successfully until 1928 when he was able to retire with a small fortune.

In the late 1890s and early 1900s my Uncle Otto was something of a popular figure in Ann Arbor, especially for the minstrel shows and barbecues that he popularized, usually in celebration of the winning football team of those years, the greatest being the "Point-a-minute" team of 1900, named for its feat of scoring an average of a point for every minute of playing time. He also boasted that he had invented the 10-yard chain marker to measure the yardage a team has to make in four downs to retain possession of the football, a device that is still in use. He was not studious himself and had little interest in intellectual concerns. He was a business man, and his first intent was always to make money, as he did. But he was also extremely generous and did not mind spending it, as I myself can witness and be grateful for.

The Ann Arbor of the first third of the twentieth century I remember well and affectionately. I lived and grew up around the old central campus. On Maynard Street I could walk through the Nichols Arcade; old Nichols was still alive, and he kept a trash and lumber yard behind his house, which was a wonder to play in at cops-and-robbers. Or I would go through my uncle's press, then through the old McClean and Neelands grocery, across State Street to Thayer Street where my uncle and aunt had their apartment. Or again on school days across the campus by the diagonal walk to the old Tappan School, where the newer engineering building now stands. That school I remember not only as the first school I attended, but the one from which the first grade teacher would dismiss me at the end of the day by giving me a kiss, to walk home then with two girls who were no less generous with their kisses on leaving me at my house.

Ann Arbor, with its university sixty years ago and more, was an exceptionally pleasant and exciting place in which to live—and also to remember!

Chapter Two

Pursuing Aristotle in Chicago

As a result of reading in mediaeval literature for my master's degree I came to two decisions that called for two radical breaks. The first was that, although the academic life was the life for me, it was not to be in the study of literature at Ann Arbor; and second, that I should enter upon the graduate study of philosophy at the University of Chicago, where a rebirth of Aristotle was occurring.

To embark upon a career in philosophy as a doctoral candidate entailed starting over again and at a considerable disadvantage. For I would be competing as a neophyte with students who had been studying philosophy intensely for several years. But this would not be the first time that I had plunged into water over my head. The same thing had already happened when I entered high school. I did not continue schooling in Ann Arbor, but instead attended a small public school located in Nogales, Arizona, on the Mexican border. My mother had died the previous year, when I was thirteen, and my father, who had been divorced when I was two years old, wanted me to live with him and his second wife and their three children. That change in itself was a shock, but little compared with the one that awaited me in high school. I entered late, some two or three weeks after the school term had begun, and was immediately placed in a class learning Spanish. Not only was this the first language other than English that I had ever heard or studied, but everyone else in the class either knew Spanish as their mother tongue or had lived with it spoken about them for their entire lives. The only advantage that I enjoyed, which was not much, was that I bothered to learn the grammar, whereas the others believed that it was unnecessary for them to do so. I never did gain any command of spoken Spanish, although I lived more or less in the midst of its Mexican version for almost three years. After returning to Nogales after fifty years to attend a school reunion, I discovered that it had become the predominant tongue, even on the Arizona side, as it had not been during my years of high school.

Going into graduate philosophy at Chicago was for me another plunge into the all but unknown. I had studied little philosophy at the University of Michigan. I took only three courses, in fact: one, an introduction, which excited no interest; another in aesthetics, which I attended largely because of my passion for poetry; and a third in Aristotle, after I had become a Catholic and a student of the Middle Ages, but neither the professor nor the students found that study exciting.

There was another more personal reason why I was attracted to Chicago. Two friends of a good friend of mine were there at the University of Chicago, participating at its very heart in the fight that seemed to be tearing the university apart over issues that at least verbally involved Aristotle and mediaevalism. From their accounts of what was taking place, Chicago was intellectually the most exciting of any university in the country.

The Hutchins-Adler Reform

Much has been written about that exciting period. The account about that period that was one of the best was given by Mortimer Adler, one of its main instigators, in his intellectual autobiography, *Philosopher at Large*. Except for providing a little background information, I will describe only the events that occurred during the year I participated in them in 1936–37.

Robert Maynard Hutchins was elected president of the University of Chicago in 1929. A year later, Hutchins brought Adler to the university as an associate professor of philosophy. The two had been associated since 1927, first in working on the law of evidence, which Hutchins taught at the Yale Law School and where he was also dean, and more recently on the theory and philosophy of education, where Adler was the moving force. In the fall of 1930 the young new president and his even younger new professor offered jointly a "General Honors Course—Readings in the classics of Western European literature", thereby launching the "Great Books Movement" at the university.

However, although great books figured largely in my year at Chicago, they do not provide the focus of what I have to say about my experience there. After all, I went to Chicago to study philosophy, and philosophy remained my main concern.

The Hutchins-Adler effort attempted and effected

many reforms in education at Chicago. Philosophically, however, the most important was the attack it made upon the "Chicago School" of philosophy. This was the title given by William James to a group led by John Dewey, who was a professor at the university in its first years, comprising George Herbert Mead and James Tufts among others. The teachings of these men had spread beyond their own department to become the reigning philosophy of the whole university. Adler wrote,

> At its very center, exercising centrifugal force, was a hard core of negations and exclusions, such as the denial of metaphysics and theology as independent of empirical science, the denial of moral values transcending adaptation to environment and escaping relativity of time and place, the denial of intellectual discipline in education.[1]

The affirmation and defense of the very opposite of these principles by Adler and Hutchins thus issued a direct challenge to the intellectual establishment of the university, not only at Chicago but throughout the United States.

The challenge was accepted. The battle was soon drawn over the issue of the hiring of new faculty members. The members of the philosophy department appointed a man of their choice and threatened to resign en masse if he was not confirmed. Hutchins refused. On a second refusal of the same sort, the philosophy faculty, aided by senior professors of other faculties, declared open revolt. The conditions, which Hutchins was compelled to accept, included acceptance of the

[1] Mortimer J. Adler, *Philosopher at Large* (New York: Macmillan, 1977), 169.

demands of the philosophy department, severe limitation on his right to make appointments to the faculty by vesting that right in the department, and the dismissal of Adler from the philosophy faculty. In July of 1931 Adler became associate professor of the philosophy of law in the Law School.

A few years later Hutchins succeeded in bringing to the faculty Richard P. McKeon, friend and colleague of Adler at Columbia, whom he had long wanted to bring to Chicago. McKeon's appointment came through regular channels, although not through the philosophy department, since he came as professor of Greek.

Another associate at New York along with McKeon was Scott Buchanan, whom Adler had known, who was not able to come until 1936, the year I was there—and then not as a regular member of any faculty. Hutchins obtained a grant from outside the university by which he was able to set up a Committee of the Liberal Arts, and Buchanan and his associate, the historian Stringfellow Barr, both of the University of Virginia, were appointed members of that committee. They, along with Adler and McKeon and younger assistants of all four men, were called upon to draw up the ideal curriculum for an undergraduate liberal arts college.

The committee as a whole held only four meetings before it was disbanded because of acrimonius disagreements among the four leading contenders. At the first meeting it was decided to read and discuss the *Poetics* of Aristotle. However, the members of the committee disagreed so strongly about the selection of the books to be read and how to read them that they agreed it was better to drop the whole idea.

All was not lost, however. The committee provided

the only reason for Buchanan's presence at the university. He then formed something of a rump session of the committee, consisting of himself, Barr, and their assistants. Together they read and discussed classical, mediaeval, and modern texts bearing on the liberal arts with the purpose of forming a college curriculum. Toward that end Buchanan composed four fascinating essays: two on tradition and the classics, one on the liberal arts proper, and one on Kant and the liberal arts. I was able to keep up with the work of the committee through my friendship with Charles Glenn Wallis, one of the assistant members and later translator of the works of Copernicus and Kepler included in Encyclopaedia Britannica's set of *Great Books of the Western World*.

However, by far that year's most important event for the development of the Great Books movement came early in 1937 when Barr learned that the centuries' old Saint John's College in Annapolis would have to close its doors unless some group capable of financing it could assume responsibility for it. Barr and Buchanan were able to form such a group, and by that summer "The New Program at St. John's College in Annapolis" was ready to begin operation under the manifesto written by Buchanan entitled "In Search of a Liberal College: A Program for the Recovery of the Classics and the Liberal Arts". However, the Saint John's story is not my story, and I write about it here mainly because of the excitement I shared by being at the edge of its formation.

Studying Philosophy

I went to Chicago, not like the young Augustine when he went to Carthage for advanced study, burning with love for love, but burning with love for Aristotle. And Aristotle I pursued. Although I was admitted as a graduate student in philosophy I did not take a single course in the philosophy department. I had no interest in "the Chicago school" of Dewey, although later on I came to know and appreciate not only William James, but even more his friend and inspirer, C. S. Peirce, and that mostly for his work in logic.

That fall of 1936 the eminent mathematical logician Rudolf Carnap had come to the philosophy department, and because he was one of the founders of Vienna's school of logical positivism I attended a few of his lectures, but I soon discovered that his kind of logic was not to my interest, and I ceased attending. That was a mistake I came to regret twenty years later. For in coming to study mediaeval logic I found that I had to learn modern mathematical logic in order to make the mediaeval thought understandable to modern readers. Hence I later faced another beginning that I could have begun in Chicago.

For the pursuit of Aristotle I enrolled in McKeon's seminar on the *De anima,* a year long course, and then in the third quarter in his course on Aristotle's *Politics.* For the reading of a philosophical text, McKeon was a great master. After an introductory lecture or two, his procedure was to call upon a student to read a sentence or so of the text and explicate it, question the student upon his explication, and then add his own comment. So he would proceed around the table of students as sentence upon sentence of the text was read. It was a slow process, and by the end of the year we had completed only about half of the *De anima,* which is not a long work. But as an introduction to the reading of Aristotle, nothing could have been better.

That seminar included students who later on made

names for themselves, including some that McKeon had brought from Columbia. There was Paul Goodman, a writer and a favorite among the "revolting young" of the 1960s, and William Barrett, later the editor of the *Partisan Review*. There was also Hippocrites Apostle, who became a translator of Aristotle's works, and about whom Bertrand Russell was rumored to have remarked that such a name was an a priori impossibility. Adler's assistant, William Gorman, who became my close friend, was also a member of that seminar.

The only "extracurricular" event that occurred in the seminar came when one of the students lost his voice and was unable to speak. He went to a psychiatrist and was told that he needed a woman. He sought relief from a prostitute and returned to the seminar a week or so later with his voice recovered, thereby revealing, it may seem, an unusual relation between vocal and sexual expression.

After a few private sessions with Adler, he suggested that I attend his undergraduate course known popularly as "The Trivium", which Buchanan was also attending. This was an honors class for pre-law students that concentrated on reading intensely and at length a few of the great books. The year that I followed it the main books were the *Physics* of Aristotle and the *De rerum natura* of Lucretius. I attended the sessions on Aristotle provided with the commentary of Saint Thomas on the *Physics,* which was also my introduction to the Thomistic commentaries on the works of Aristotle.

I also took a course in the music department given by Herbert Schwartz in which he applied the principles of Aristotle's *Poetics* to a piece by Mozart. Schwartz had been trained as a youth to become a concert pianist, but had decided he lacked the talent or the desire to pursue such a career and instead had turned to philosophy. He took the Ph.D. degree at Columbia under McKeon with a dissertation on the *Poetics* with special application to music. At Chicago he had to teach in the music department inasmuch as that was one of the departments that would accept appointments at Hutchins' suggestion.

Catholic Excitement

At the University of Chicago I became associated for the first time in my life with a group of students who were enthusiastically Catholic. Oddly enough, most of them were converts of an even more recent vintage than I was. The Aristotelian revival there had also extended into the study of Saint Thomas Aquinas, and Adler himself was deep into it, including close association with the Dominicans, many of whom considered themselves the keeper of the saint, who was one of their order. Among the students, undergraduate as well as graduate, there was sufficient interest in reading the text of Saint Thomas that the Dominicans at their House of Studies in River Forest sent one of their professors down to the parish church of Saint Thomas the Apostle to conduct a weekly course in the *Summa theologica*. There, under Fr. Timothy Sparks, O.P., I began my first systematic reading of the Angelic Doctor with a priest as angelic as his master.

During the 1930s there were many conversions to the Catholic Church. Among those I knew personally were Kenneth "Bud" Simon, an M.D. from Ann Arbor, who studied psychiatry at Chicago and after becoming Catholic went on to become a Cistercian priest; Herbert Ratner, also an M.D. from Ann Arbor, who later became health commissioner of Oak Park, Illinois, and founding editor of the magazine *Child and Family;* Winston Ashley, who became a Dominican priest; John Oesterle and his wife, Jean, who became professors of philosophy at Notre Dame and Saint Mary's College; Margaret Stern; and Alice Zucker.

For those very fruitful years for the Church at the University of Chicago, the one exerting the most direct personal influence was undoubtedly Herbert Schwartz. He became intensely religious and, after his own conversion, his own enthusiasm reached out to others. After a few years of teaching, including a time at the new program of Saint John's, Annapolis, he became in effect the lay abbot of a religious community that included many priests.

A Contemporary Assessment

The year 1936–37 proved to be an *annus mirabilis* for me. That year in which I first studied under Mortimer Adler led to a life-time association and turned out to be at least practically the single most important year in my intellectual and professional life. Out of it came my work with him on the compilation of the *Syntopicon* of great ideas that serves as an analytical index to the set of *Great Books of the Western World* published by Encyclopaedia Britannica, Inc.—then on to my becoming a fellow of his Institute for Philosophical Research; editor of *The Great Ideas Today,* the annual volume published for subscribers to the set of great books; and an associate in preparing the *Propaedia,* the outline of the world of knowledge that prepared the new edition of the *Encyclopaedia Britannica* of 1972 and forms its first volume. And finally through his influence with Fr. John J. Cavanaugh, C.S.C., the president of the University of Notre Dame, to my becoming the founder of the Great Books program at Notre Dame, which still continues strong. My association with Mortimer Adler still continues also, fifty-four years after it began in 1937.

At the conclusion of that year in Chicago I wrote a long letter to my friend Craig LaDrière, whom I had come to know while he was gaining his doctorate degree in Ann Arbor and had then become a Junior Fellow at Harvard; later he became professor of literary theory at Catholic University and then at Harvard. Since the letter sums up my experience of living through those heady days at the University of Chicago, it can count as a little "historical document" of those times.

Friday 16th July 1937
... I would write, what I have already promised in an earlier letter, a little history of my year at Chicago; which I trust will be of interest to you at the same time it will furnish me the occasion for a little "stock-taking".

But before I begin I would like to add a few words, by way of preface, on the matter and the method I shall use. As I shall attempt to tell my story in terms of the liberal arts, I shall, of course, be accused of telling my story of Chicago in the jargon of Chicago, for at least superficially it will appear so. But I would remind you of the dichotomy established at Chicago between Grammar and Logic, between being "literary" and being "philosophical"—"literary" being derogatory and a term of abuse. With this distinction it will at once be clear that although my tongue may be strange and sounding at times to the tune of the Chicago Logic, the story I tell and the means I use are "literary", not "philosophical". I hope to profit and delight by the charm of the analogical insofar as I succeed in analogizing the arts to my year's experience by means of personalities, which on any account is a very "literary" thing to do; in fact, hasn't someone defined literature as only a refined gossip? . . .

In order to locate the matrix, as it were, of my discussion I shall designate the major personalities according to the trivial arts each is most practised in; and at the same time chart the plot of my tale, inasmuch as the beginning, middle, and end will be determined respectively according to the personality and the art that each signifies. In Adler I find the best dialectician, the one of those at Chicago who best may stand for Logic; McKeon is the best scholar among the philosophers there inasmuch as he is the best grammarian, and he may fittingly represent Grammar; while Buchanan is probably the only gentleman of the three, the only literary person there, and his art is properly Rhetoric. My *itinerarium mentis* of the year, as I look back upon it now, was from Logic through Grammar to Rhetoric; and as far as I can see ahead now, I shall probably devote myself to persuading young minds of the validity of the Middle Ages.

As you know, it was Herbert Schwartz who got me to go to Chicago, and as he is with Adler rather than either of the other two "personalities", I can say that it was Logic that lured me there. I went to learn dialectic, much to Reinhard's disgust, dialectic having died in the 16th century according to his way of thinking. Conscious of my lack in critical thought, I went to acquire that discipline in philosophy, without which one can't go far in literature, or in anything for that matter. And as I was under the influence of Herbert, who would excel in dialectic above all else, my first quarter passed in philosophy under the direction of Herbert and Adler with the emphasis on dialectic. I gained some knowledge of the problems of philosophy and followed Adler as he criticized modern philosophy and science by reducing their position to that of the pre-Socratics and then subjecting them to the Aristotelian criticism. But more important than that I learned the scholastic terminology of philosophy and acclimated myself to that atmosphere filled with talk of the four causes, potency and act, form and matter, and the rest of it, which you have already got wind of in Harvard. It was a necessary work, necessary as an introduction to any further study of Aristotle and the schoolmen, and Adler is the finest at Chicago for that sort of thing. He has an extremely facile mind, is a genius at outlines, and has the history of philosophy at his finger tips (it has galvanized in his mind, as Buchanan says), so that it is only a matter of a moment for him to state his problem, analyze it, and explain its terms, and offer a solution—all in the best of the etiquette laid down by his master Aristotle. And yet for all the excellences of his gift, inasmuch as he was offering a course in the reading of a text, and not one in Special Problems, he wasn't too successful in teaching the *Physics*. It is really misleading to say he was working on a text, for a text for Adler is only a spring-board from which he takes off into the problems of philosophy and the modern world. It is all very exciting while it lasts, but afterwards, on remembering the subject is the *Physics,* it seems something of a frost; and one wonders why the text is mentioned at all or the course offered as one in the reading of the text. . . . The matter is there for making the best course in the country. No university could do better, for instance, than a course in the *Physics* in which McKeon taught the first quarter by giving a strict grammatical reading of the first book; Adler taking the second, raising the problems of physics and giving the Aristotelian solution, while Buchanan would take the third quarter and polish off the year's work by pointing out the importance and fixing the place of the *Physics* in the realm of human knowledge—giving a literary and cultural twist to it, as it were. . . .

It wasn't until the second quarter was on its way that I got to appreciate and profit from the teaching of McKeon. Now I'm not so sure that I didn't profit most of all from him, for I think I can truly say I learned to read from his courses in the *De anima* and the *Politics*. We spent the entire year on the *De anima* and at that only finished about half of it, and it isn't a long book, as you know, only about 100 pages. But from that I found out how to approach a book and derive at least a good literal meaning from it. McKeon orders a text much as St. Thomas does, but to a much greater degree; he accounts for every word whereas Thomas will work with sentences. He has that reverence for a text, granting that it is a text worth reading, that compels him to read it well and to make sense out of it, something nowadays all too rare, for if a passage prove difficult we only too often ascribe it to "corruptions in the text" without attempting to grapple with the meaning. The criticism of modern scholars on the *Politics* is an excellent example of this, for they think the *Politics* is the worst Aristotelian text that has come down to us. They have even gone so far as to find the traditional order of the books all wrong, and now there are many different arrangements of the books "as they should be". McKeon, however, not only believes that the traditional order is the correct one, but proves it to be so without a possible doubt; for knowing Aristotle as a whole, he knows the Aristotelian method, and with that he finds an order that can't be other than from beginning to middle to end. Aristotle is difficult, and without a good grammatical and logical training one can't very well understand what he is driving at. But the scholars I know of don't even avail themselves of the tools there are at hand. They are not only weak in discipline, but don't even know of the great tradition of Aristotelian commentators. . . .

However, McKeon has limited his own powers by his concentration on Grammar. In teaching an Aristotelian text he assumes the mask of Aristotle, and the problems are raised not for the sake of the truth, but in order to see what Aristotle's solution of it is. This attitude of his had developed so fully even while he was a student that Gilson is supposed to have said that he was killing his philosophy with Grammar. . . . I think one can pose the issue between him and Adler as that old fight of Grammar versus Logic, though one must remember that here it is a question of method and not of subject matter. Both are philosophers and, with different emphasis, Aristotelians. . . .

[Buchanan] is too "literary" for the Chicago group . . . his literary extravagance being shown in his acceptance of culture as a religion. He will excuse himself by saying that the fault is not in him but in his stars, and then go on to sacramentalize education, substituting the classics for the Scriptures and the liberal arts for the Sacraments. He has made some very penetrating observations on education by means of this analogy, but to accept only one side of the analogy is to erect a vicious fiction. We must, however, admit that analogizing the liberal arts to the Sacraments is an excellent rhetorical device; if Catholics could be persuaded to see the validity of the analogy, a large step would be made towards "doing something" about Catholic education. So it is no exaggeration to say Buchanan excels in Rhetoric.

This letter was written fifty-four years ago when I was twenty-three years old, and it reveals more of my own attitudes at the time than anything it says about its ostensible subjects. I was extremely "bookish", and although I have continued to appreciate the close reading of a text such as McKeon practiced it, I came to see after becoming a teacher that there is great value in Adler's method. It puts the emphasis upon what the book is about rather than upon the book itself. Hence attention is directed toward the truth of things rather than toward the mastery of a book. Of course, it is a matter of justice to give the author the best reading that can be achieved.

As is obvious from the letter, it was at Chicago that I became intensely interested in the theory and history of the liberal arts. In fact, the first research project I undertook on completing the doctoral degree was in the history of the liberal arts in the Middle Ages. Out of this work there came many years later some papers on the development of mediaeval logic and a book dealing with the philosophy of the humanities, about both of which I will have more to say.

I left the University of Chicago after one academic year. But I had got a hold upon Aristotle, which was my main reason for going there, and it was a hold that would become stronger as I continued to study his works with the help of the commentaries of Saint Thomas. My main purpose, however, both intellectually and academically remained the search for the Middle Ages.

Chapter Three

Finding the Middle Ages in Toronto

During the year that I was in Chicago I was persuaded by my Catholic friends that the best place to study the Middle Ages, at least on the North American continent, was at the University of Toronto. There a few years previously one of the great authorities on mediaeval thought, Professor Etienne Gilson of the Collège de France, had established with the Basilian Fathers the Institute of Mediaeval Studies. There, with mind and heart set to that end, I was determined to go. As further preparation for gaining acceptance, I enrolled in the spring quarter in the course of Latin Paleography offered by Professor Charles H. Beeson, where I was once again a neophyte. This, along with the study of Aristotle I had done at Chicago and of mediaeval literature at Ann Arbor, qualified me for acceptance as an advanced graduate student in the Institute, where I was "incepted" in the fall of 1937.

The Institute had been established as the graduate arm of Saint Michael's College within the University of Toronto, one of the five autonomous colleges comprising the university. This college arrangement provided and still does provide special advantages in that it makes it possible for a student to belong to a relatively small college—either Catholic, Anglican, Presbyterian, United Church, or secular—and yet still enjoy the facilities of a large university. Gilson had been invited by Harvard University to set up his Institute in Cambridge. But he preferred to do so with the Basilians in Toronto, where, I suspect, he knew he could wield more power with less interference and perhaps also feel more at home. Indeed, the Institute and its library have become in part a living memorial to Gilson, to his direction as well as to his vast achievement in the study, analysis, and exposition of the thought of the Middle Ages.

The Institute of Mediaeval Studies

Since I intend to tell here how I found the Middle Ages in Toronto while obtaining a doctoral degree in philosophy, I must write at some length about the Institute. For except for a single course in Kant, all my class work during the two years from 1937 to 1939 was done at the Institute. This task is both easier and more rewarding in that Fr. Laurence Shook, in his biography of Gilson,[1] has told much of the history of the Institute, and that, along with my own experience there, provides the source of my account.

The Institute of the late 1930s was a far different place than what it has since become. Throughout the years since its opening in 1929 it has continued to train students in the life and thought of the Middle Ages. But during my years there, the place was a veritable nest of fledgling

---

[1] Laurence K. Shook, *Etienne Gilson* (Toronto: Pontifical Institute of Mediaeval Studies, 1984).

philosophers, the great majority of whom went on to become academic teachers of philosophy. The attraction exercised by Gilson and Jacques Maritain as its principal teachers may well account for the call that the students answered. Both Gilson and Maritain spent part of each year in Toronto, but Gilson much more regularly and for longer periods. He divided his year between his work in Toronto and work in Paris at the Collège de France and the Académie française. At the Institute he was much more influential than Maritain in directing and participating in its teaching and research.

Soon after arriving at the Institute I discovered that its students in typical fashion tended to divide into two groups, one of which considered themselves followers of Maritain in being primarily interested in speculative philosophy while the other consisted of followers of Gilson in having a major interest in historical scholarship. I thought that such a division was false and artificial, since Gilson was certainly a philosopher as well as a historical scholar. But this judgment of mine was immediately interpreted as indicating that I was at heart a Gilsonian. And so I was. Not out of any disrespect for Maritain, from whom I learned much and whom I both admired and respected. But mostly because the Institute as a whole, in inspiration, origin, and direction, was the work of Gilson, established for the study of the Middle Ages, and that study was then my goal.

Maritain, as is evident even from photographs of him, was in physical appearance both aesthetic and spiritual, whereas Gilson looked more like a French baker or butcher. But in thought, speech, and writing, Gilson was beautifully lucid and graceful, and as lecturer, teacher, and seminar director, he was simply superb.

The Institute as Gilson conceived and wrought it was a highly specialized one. But its specialty was not philosophy, not Thomism, but the entire field of mediaeval studies. His inspiration for such a research center seems to have come from two colleagues of his when he was at the University of Strasbourg in the 1920s: the two historians Lucien Febvre and Marc Bloch. Through their journal *Les annales d'histoire économique et sociales* they brought about the rise of a new school of historiography that has come to be known as the Annales school. They proclaimed the need for a total history of man in all his aspects that would break down the walls erected by the specialized disciplines whose results are at best only partial histories. Gilson considered himself first and foremost a professional historian. But history for him was conceived in this total sense, and it was from the work of Febvre and Bloch that Gilson first begin to see all that would be required for a study of the Middle Ages entire. As Father Shook wrote:

> He began, in short, to dream of his own institute where all medieval studies might be taught and researched in an integrated fashion, where philosophy, and theology, history, literature, and so on, could be pursued as related disciplines. Here the various branches of study could share their methodologies, both traditional and new. Why could not Aquinas, or Abelard, or Augustine, read with the precision of Bloch's scrutiny of the works of man, provide insights into humanities and civilization beyond anything yet achieved?[2]

Gilson's aim, as he once succintly put it, was to make the students of the Institute connatural with all that they would meet in reading Dante.

[2] Ibid., 95.

The result of endeavoring to achieve that ideal was a highly specialized research and teaching center. Yet it was also one that was highly integrated and general in that it refused to limit itself by concentrating upon any single specialized discipline. Instead it required the study of all matters and methods pertinent to understanding the Middle Ages. Even before founding the Institute, Gilson was working to breach the walls that separate the specialized disciplines from one another. In launching with Père G. Théry of the Saulchoir Seminary the research journal *Archives d'histoire doctrinale et littéraire du moyen age,* he put forward "a publication dedicated to healing the rift between the history of medieval thought and the history of medieval letters".

Hence it is not surprising that a candidate who aspired to receive the Licenciate from the Institute had to take and pass a required set of courses. In my day the course of studies was "so arranged that in the first year the student receives a general view of the whole field of Mediaeval Studies". Once that was completed, he had to choose a field of specialization. But "to avoid a too narrow specialization", it was further specified that "the student must, during the second and third year, take a certain number of courses from the other sections".

Graduate Study

When I entered, as already noted, I had completed two years of graduate study largely in the mediaeval field, and I was accordingly given credit for the study I had done in literature, philosophy, and paleography. Then for lack of time and money I did not pursue the full Licentiate but took the shorter route to the Ph.D. degree in philosophy granted by the University of Toronto.

Even so, my studies at the Institute covered a fairly wide range. I did two years of reading the Provençal troubadours with Father Denomy, a year of Patristics with Father Muckle, and two years of Saint Thomas with Father Phelan. This last consisted of studying the *Commentary on the De interpretatione* of Aristotle, the *Quaestio de anima,* the theory of the concept and of the habits that provide the basis for a philosophy of education. Capping all came Gilson's lectures and seminar, and a short series by Maritain on education.

Gilson's lectures gave the results of his current research. During the fall term he delivered the lectures in English in Toronto and then in the spring in Paris, and these lectures were frequently reworked and published later in book form. The first series that I attended in 1937 was on "The Mediaeval Background of Realism", and this series provided the basis for the book he published two years later under the title *Réalism thomiste et critique de de la connaissance.* In 1938 he lectured on "The History of Christian Social Philosophy", lectures which eventually were worked into the book *Les metamorphoses de la cité de Dieu* (1952). The principal series seldom consisted of more than eight or ten lectures a term, given at weekly intervals. He demanded time for research so as to allow free rein to his great scholarly energy and productiveness. When offered a post at the University of California, Berkeley, at a handsome salary, he was appalled to learn that he would be required to meet at least twelve periods a week, and he refused to sacrifice time for money.

The research seminar that I participated in was devoted to Saint Augustine and Plotinus. Six months or so before the first seminar we were informed of the topic to be

Finding the Middle Ages in Toronto

studied and advised to start preparing for it. I accordingly acquired the works of Plotinus (in the Budé Greek-French edition) and spent several months reading them. At the first seminar, Gilson discussed the subject for research and assigned topics for the papers that the students were to prepare and present. In this case we were to take the words of Saint Augustine in the *Confessions,* where he tells of what he learned from his reading of the Platonists (that is, Plotinus), of what helped him on his way to Christianity, and of what did not. Here is the text that Gilson read from the *Confessions* (bk. VII.ix.13–14), as translated by E. B. Pusey:

> And Thou, willing first to show me how Thou *resistest the proud, but givest grace unto the humble,* and by how great an act of Thy Mercy Thou hadst traced out to men the way of humility, in that Thy WORD was made flesh, and dwelt among men:—Thou procuredst for me, by means of one puffed up with most unnatural pride, certain books of the Platonists, translated from Greek into Latin. And therein I read, not indeed in the very words, but to the very same purpose, enforced by many and divers reasons, that *In the beginning was the Word, and the Word was with God, and the Word was God: the Same was in the beginning with God: all things were made by Him, and without Him was nothing made: that which was made by Him is life, and the life was the light of men, and the light shineth in the darkness, and the darkness comprehended it not.* And that the soul of man, though it *bears witness to the light,* yet itself *is not that light;* but the Word of God, being God, *is that true light that lighteth every man that cometh into the world.* And that *He was in the world, and the world was made by Him, and the world knew Him not.* But that *He came unto His own, and His own received Him not, but as many as received Him, to them gave*

He power to become the sons of God, as many as believed in His name, this I read not there.

Again I read there, that *God the Word was born not of flesh, nor of blood, nor of the will of man, nor of the will of the flesh, but of God.* But that *the Word was made flesh, and dwelt among us,* I read not there. For I traced in those books that it was many and divers ways said, that *the Son was in the form of the Father, and thought it not robbery to be equal with God,* for that naturally He was the Same Substance. But that *He emptied himself, taking the form of a servant, being made in the likeness of men, and found in fashion as a man, humbled Himself, and became obedient unto death, and that the death of the cross: wherefore God exalted Him* from the dead *and gave Him a name above every name, that at the name of Jesus every knee should bow, of things in heaven, and things in earth, and things under the earth; and that every tongue should confess that the Lord Jesus Christ is in the Glory of God the Father;* those books have not. For that before all times and above all times Thy Only-Begotten Son remaineth unchangeable, co-eternal with Thee, and that *of His fulness souls receive,* that they may be blessed; and that by participation of wisdom abiding in them, they are renewed, so as to be wise, is there. But that *in due time He died for the ungodly;* and that *Thou sparedst not Thine Only Son, but deliveredst Him for us all,* is not there. *For Thou hiddest these things from the wise, and revealedst them to babes;* that they *that labour and are heavy laden might come unto Him, and He refresh them,* because *He is meek and lowly in heart, and the meek He directeth in judgment, and the gentle He teacheth His ways, beholding our loneliness and trouble, and forgiving all our sins.* But such as are lifted up in the lofty walk of some would-be sublimer learning, hear not Him, saying, *Learn of Me, for I am meek and lowly in heart, and ye shall find rest to your souls. Although they knew God, yet they glorify*

Him not as God, nor are thankful, but was vain in their thoughts; and their foolish heart is darkened; professing that they were wise, they became fools.[3]

Gilson divided this text so as to provide a separate topic for each member of the seminar to take as the subject of the paper he was to write. I took the first one and for the next week worked furiously to show how, from the writings of Plotinus, Augustine could claim that he had learned that "In the beginning was the Word, and the Word was with God, and the Word was God". I then had to read my paper before Gilson, who was seated at one end of a long table, I at the other end, and the students along the sides. Gilson would listen carefully, interrupt now and then with a few comments, but reserve until the second hour, after the reading had been completed, his main criticism. Then, of course, the trial and judgment began in earnest. It could prove to be difficult and uncomfortable if he found that you had failed to prove your thesis from the best sources. To my great relief, I had not fallen into disaster.

A Dissertation on Cavalcanti

Meantime, besides following my various courses, I was also at work on my dissertation. Here I was extremely fortunate, doubly so, as it turned out. Gilson, at the instigation of T. S. Eliot, had reviewed for the latter's journal, *The Criterion,* the study and edition that the

---

[3] *The Confessions of St. Augustine* (London: J. M. Dent & Sons, 1932), 129–32.

poet Ezra Pound had made of Guido Cavalcanti, the mediaeval Italian poet. The edition included photographs of an early commentary in Latin on Cavalcanti's most famous and difficult poem that begins with the words "Donna mi priega" ("A Lady asks me"). Pound, in an introductory essay, had ventured an interpretation of the poem. Gilson, in his generous review, suggested that if Pound was sincerely interested in understanding the difficult poem, he should start by studying the early commentary that he knew about. Pound no sooner read the review than he mailed off his photostats of the commentary to Gilson and told him to get to work. Gilson's work on it consisted in depositing the photostats of the commentary in the Institute, where they remained as though awaiting my arrival.

Thus I came upon and inherited, as it were, an ideal dissertation topic. I was studying both mediaeval literature and philosophy, and here at hand was a commentary on a famous mediaeval Italian poem on the nature of love, written by a poet, friend of Dante, and known for his knowledge of natural philosophy. The commentary was written in Latin by Dino del Garbo, a professor of medicine in Bologna and Florence, and hence himself learned in the natural philosophy of the Middle Ages. There was but one known manuscript of the Latin commentary written in Italy, which made the paleographical problem easier. I needed only to edit the manuscript, translate it into English, and provide my own commentary by way of locating sources in mediaeval philosophical texts that would throw light upon the meaning of the fourteenth century commentary. I had the still further good fortune in finding that the Italian department of the University of Toronto had as one of its professors

J. E. Shaw, who was himself especially interested in the Cavalcanti poem, who had studied it long, and with whom I had many valuable discussions. He later produced a book entitled *Guido Cavalcanti's Theory of Love* (1949).

Cavalcanti's poem begins with the words, as translated into English,

> A lady asks me that I would tell
> of an accident which is often fierce
> and is so great that it is called love.

The poem then goes on to list the questions about love that the lady would like to have answered, namely:

> where it is posited and who makes it created,
> and what its virtue is and its power,
> its essence and its every movement,
> the pleasingness which makes it called loving,
> and whether one can show it by sight.[4]

In the answers the poet gave to these questions in the body of the poem he drew upon the common philosophical and scientific teachings of his age about the passions, which is one of the causes of the poem's difficulty. His commentator, Dino del Garbo, doctor of medicine, explicated many of these. My task in writing a commentary upon the commentary was to provide still further elucidation of the teachings that might lie behind the poem. I was thus able to draw together my own interest and work not only in philosophy and literature, but

---

[4] Otto Bird, "The Canzone d'Amore of Cavalcanti according to the Commentary of Dino del Garbo", in *Mediaeval Studies* 2 (1940): 157.

also that which I had done at Ann Arbor on the mediaeval love lyric.

Candidates for the Ph.D. degree often are paralyzed by the dissertation that is required, which is supposed to be an original contribution to the field of knowledge in which it lies. Hence many become only Ph.D.'s that are A.B.D.'s ("All but dissertation"). I had no such ill fortune. In fact, the research that my dissertation required provided one of the most intellectually satisfying episodes in my life.

After the dissertation I published no further research papers in mediaeval thought until more than twenty years later. I then became interested in logic when a number of distinguished logicians lectured at the University of Notre Dame, including the historians I. M. Bochenski from Poland and Switzerland and Ivo Thomas from England, both of whom were Dominican priests. Under their influence I returned to research into mediaeval matters.

I concentrated upon the subject of the logical Topics (*topoi* in Greek, *loci* in Latin). Aristotle had written the first treatise on them, in fact the longest of his logical writings, in which about three hundred of them were identified and analyzed. The subject continued to be of logical interest throughout antiquity, and Boethius left a treatise on it. Then with the recovery of logic in the Middle Ages, the Topics provided the material for one of the treatises in the standard manuals of logic and continued to do so from the time of Abelard down to the Renaissance.

A Topic is a "place" where arguments may be found, in that it provides a general rule or warrant capable of validating any number of particular arguments. Take, for example, the Topic concerning genus and species, which can be stated thus:

> Of whatever the species is predicated,
> the genus is also predicated.

This particular Topic warrants such particular arguments as the following:

> Socrates is a man, therefore Socrates is an animal.
> He who describes a circle is one who describes
> a figure.
> If the cloth is red, the cloth is colored.

The Topic warrants the argument because the relation between man-animal, circle-figure, and red-color is in each case that of species-genus. Since the relation of the terms here has to be known as that of species to genus, the argument is extra- or non-formal in the logical sense. However, it is possible to render the Topics, or some of them, as strictly formal, and it was this "formalization" of them that the mediaeval logicians were concerned about. Thus, for example, the Topic of Genus-Species can be formalized as follows:

> *If A is included in B,*
> *then for all D,*
> if *D* is included in *A,* then *D* is included in *B.*

And this as so stated is a law of strictly formal logic, and for the mediaeval logicians as well as for Bertrand Russell, who proves it so in his *Principia Mathematica,* where it appears as a proposition (+ 37.2) and is attributed to the teacher of Leibniz.[5]

---

[5] Alfred North Whitehead and Bertrand Russell, *Principia Mathematica* (Cambridge, Eng.: University Press, 1950), 1:283–84.

I have long since ceased to do any work on the Topics. However, the few papers I published on the subject provided the idea for a doctoral dissertation by Professor Eleonore Stump, and she has gone on in further books and papers greatly to extend understanding of logic in the Middle Ages.

The "Aeterni Patris"

The central and most important outcome from my years at Toronto was neither the doctoral degree nor the research. Rather it was the discovery of my intellectual home in philosophy and theology. This too I owed to the Institute. In addition to its comprehensive approach to mediaeval studies there was another way in which its program was general in an integrative way. This came from the particular emphasis that was given to the writings and thought of Saint Thomas Aquinas.

My course work, as I have already noted, concentrated greatly on the text of Saint Thomas, where it counted toward my degree as a "concentration in systematic philosophy", despite the fact that Thomas had no "system", as Gilson insisted. However, in addition to this the Institute had another reason, which became apparent in the first course in the history of philosophy that I was required to take. It was devoted to the study by Siger de Brabant, the opponent of Thomas at the University of Paris, on the eternity of the world. But before turning to that text we made a careful study of the "Aeterni Patris", the encyclical letter that Pope Leo XIII issued in 1879 that called for the "restoring in Christian schools of Christian philosophy according to the angelic mind of St. Thomas Aquinas".[6]

I do not know who was responsible for this requirement. Perhaps it was the Basilian fathers of Saint Michael's College. Father Shook reports that the college "tried to implement 'Aeterni Patris' and strengthened its department of philosophy in the 1920s" by appointing to its faculty such Thomists as De Wulf, Noel, Phelan, and "then after 1926 by aggressively pursuing Gilson". Gilson himself thought highly of Leo XIII, as is evident from the loving edition he made of the encyclicals that form *The Social Teachings of Pope Leo XIII* (1954). Yet he had little sympathy for the philosophers at the University of Louvain and the Institut catholique at Paris, who had done the most by the 1920s to put into practice the recommendations of the pope.

The plea and recommendation of the "Aeterni Patris" rests on two major principles. First, that there exists a Christian philosophy with a definite position on the relation between faith and reason, between Christianity and philosophy; and second, that the best and soundest expression of Christian philosophy is to be found in the writings of Saint Thomas Aquinas.

With regard to the first principle, the letter argued at some length for the consonance and consilience of Christianity with philosophy to the mutual benefit of both. As evidence of this, the Pope cited the writing

---

[6] Leo XIII, encyclical letter "Aeterni Patris", translated as "On Christian Philosophy", in *The Church Speaks to the Modern World: The Social Teachings of Leo XIII,* ed. Etienne Gilson (Garden City, N.Y.: Doubleday, 1954), 29–54.

of Saint Justin Martyr among the Apologists, of Saint Augustine among the Fathers, and of Saint Thomas and Saint Bonaventure among the Scholastics. With regard to Saint Thomas, in calling for the recovery and restoration of his teaching in the schools, the pope emphasized that this work should be done by the study of the text of Saint Thomas itself.

Pope Leo's strong defense of Aquinas in 1879 started and encouraged a movement that resulted not only in the recovery of his writings through the publication of many editions of them, but also in a closer study and a better understanding of the whole of mediaeval thought. Gilson's own prodigious efforts in that field may be considered themselves as a response to that call.

The Institute acted on the recommendation by making the work of Saint Thomas the center of its philosophy and theology. In so doing it accomplished a double purpose. In that teaching it obtained an integrating principle of unity for all of its studies, and at the same time it acquired a perennial source of enlightenment with which to address the problems of the contemporary world. The graduate of the Institute would be prepared for teaching and research in the field of mediaeval studies, which in itself would amount to a considerable achievement. But then in addition to this, by being grounded in the principles of Saint Thomas he would be prepared as a Catholic Christian to meet and deal with the issues that he would face in the world. Acknowledgment of the Institute's work in these respects was officially recognized in 1937 when by papal bull it was declared to be a Papal Institute.

Saint Thomas Aquinas

Thomas Aquinas is known with good reason as the Angelic Doctor. An angel, as he taught, has a purely intellectual nature, and the writings of Thomas reveal a human intellect approaching as closely as it possibly can to that of the angel. He is also the *Doctor Communis,* the teacher of all Catholic schools. In his teaching he stands in close association with two other saints, Saint Paul and Saint Augustine. These three teachers are preeminently the great saints of reconciliation in that each of them endeavored and succeeded in bringing together diverse and different intellectual traditions. Saint Paul brought to his Christian teaching the whole religious tradition of ancient Israel. Saint Augustine had behind his work not only Saint Paul, but also the literary humanistic culture of classical antiquity as well as one of its great philosophical traditions, that of Plato and Plotinus. And Saint Thomas had behind his teaching not only the work of both Saint Paul and Saint Augustine, but also the great monastic contribution of the Middle Ages as well as the other great philosophical tradition of antiquity, that of Aristotle.

Since the thirteenth century there have been great and glorious intellectual achievements. But there have been no thinkers of reconciliation to equal in stature these three saints. Indeed, the very thought of reconciliation and synthesis in the intellectual order has been spurned as an ideal. Our teachers, especially the philosophers, have preferred to start anew; or they have chosen sides and divided the intellectual world rather than attempting to unite it; or else, saddest of all, each has been content "to do his own thing".

The work of reconciliation for which Thomas is best known is that of accomodating and converting the philosophical wisdom of Aristotle to the supernatural wisdom of the Christian faith. He succeeded in winning Aristotle from the great Arab thinkers who until then had been Aristotle's keepers. Figuratively speaking, he persuaded the Greek pagan philosopher to accept baptism and so become a champion of the Church. Yet Thomas' work did not stop here. Aristotle represented the high point of the new learning that was flooding and endangering the Christendom of the time, challenging the old learning and especially the supremacy of Augustine. The result was the outbreak of an intense and often bitter quarrel between ancients and moderns. At the time Thomas was identified as a proponent of the moderns. He was not only expert in the new learning, especially that of Aristotle, but he also used all the latest teaching methods and in many cases improved upon them. In fact, his first biographers stressed the novelty of his teaching: "New arrangements of the subject-matter, new methods of proof, new arguments adduced for the conclusions."[7] Yet it was also recognized, as we see so well today, that Thomas cannot be identified simply with that of the moderns. His writing reveals the conviction and determination not to allow any truth once acquired to perish and be lost to human use. Thus

---

[7] Bernard Gui, "Life", in Kenelm Foster, *The Life of Saint Thomas Aquinas, Biographical Documents* (London: Longmans, Green Co., 1959).

with respect to the intellectual tradition, he was a giant champion of the cause of the ancients.

As I read, taught, and reread his work, my devotion to Saint Thomas increased and with it also came a better understanding of the Christian faith. He began his greatest work, the *Summa theologiae,* with a consideration of *sacra doctrina*. These words are usually translated as "sacred doctrine", but they could equally well be taken as "holy teaching", and this way perhaps better emphasizes the holiness of his work. There are at least three distinct ways in which his teaching deserves to be called holy. First, teaching consists in an action—the action of who is causing knowledge. But the knowledge with which Thomas is dealing in the *Summa* is no less than the action of God himself, the Holy of Holies, teaching men through faith in his revelation. Hence, the teaching is holy because God is its first principle and source. Second, it is holy also because of its content—because of what is taught—which is devoted to God and the things of God. Third, this teaching is holy in the way that food or medicine is healthy in that it is a cause of holiness as the others are of health.

Our aim, indeed our very happiness, does not consist merely in learning about divine things. Beyond that, it consists in the actual experience of them. But the experience of God and of divine things does not come from a mere intellectual grasp of a scientific theology. It comes from loving God and his ways and cleaving to them by affection. It was through such teaching as this that Thomas became saintly, and his teaching can help to work the same wonder in ourselves.

The feature of his teaching that makes it especially

saintly appears in his central metaphysical intuition, a truth he emphasized in his first work and continued to do thereafter. That there is something rather than nothing—that fact is the great cause of wonder for Thomas as well as for Leibniz and in our own day for Heidegger, who remarked: "Man alone of all existing things . . . experiences the wonder of all wonders: that there are things-in-being."[8] Wherever we look there are indeed things-in-being, and not nothing. Yet we also find, as Saint Augustine did, that when we ask them whether they made themselves, one and all answer unanimously that they did not make themselves, that they are not the cause of their own being, but received it from another. Thus, according to the teaching of Thomas, wherever there is anything at all God must be present there as the giver of its existence.

The wonder that there is something rather than nothing is capable of generating a spirit of reverence. In fact, the affirmation that something is, hence any and every true statement that we make, contains implicitly an affirmation of God. Such openness to being led Thomas to assert and emphasize the value of every being as being. In doing so, he countered and corrected the excessive supernaturalism of some of his predecessors, who were so intent upon the search for God that they tended to view all natural things of this world as shadows, images, and symbols of God and the supernatural. The teaching of Thomas provides a secure basis for recognizing the rights and privileges of natural being, and hence that creatures, and man especially, are a source

---

[8] Martin Heidegger, "What is Metaphysics", in *Existence and Being*, ed. Werner Brock (Chicago: Henry Regnery, 1949), 355.

and seat of values in themselves. Thomas asserted the rights and power of nature so strongly that in his own day he was sometimes accused by his critics of abandoning Christ for Aristotle.

Aquinas, however, was no nature worshipper. The spirit of wonder at and reverence and gratitude for existence does sometimes confound the existence of the creature with that of the Creator and result in a misty kind of pantheism. To the ancients all things were full of gods, and it has been a prime task of Christianity from the beginning to desacralize or secularize the world of the divinities that have been attributed to it. Against the pagans the early Christian Fathers, like their Jewish teachers, asserted that God is one and there is no God but God. In the *City of God,* Augustine in effect secularized Roman history so as to remove the aura of divinity that had surrounded it by reducing it to human dimensions. Thomas continued along the same line by desacralizing nature. The clear distinction that he made between the existential structure of creatures and that of God makes it impossible for anyone who follows his teaching to confuse the creature with its Creator.

Thomas in all of his writings is impersonal, intellectualistic, Aristotelian, and scholastic, and all of it manifests signs of the classroom. This is true even of his commentaries on Sacred Scripture. His commentary on Job, for example, has been described as portraying Job as engaging in a scholastic disputation of the sort that was common practice at the University of Paris in the thirteenth century. These features of his writings have misled some readers into identifying his teaching with the form in which it is presented. But nothing could be more false, as is evident from the complete transformation he gave to the ethical ideal of Aristotle.

Thomas drew strongly upon the ethical writings of Aristotle, used them in his theological work, but redirected them to an entirely different end. The happiness of man, he taught, depends upon that which directs him most efficaciously toward the source of all being and of all good, which is God. But given the human situation in this life, we can love God more than we can know him. Indeed, the best knowledge that we can have of him here is the dark knowledge of faith. Yet we can love God with all that we are and all that we have: "with all [our] heart, with all [our] soul, with all [our] mind, and with all [our] strength" (Mk 12:30–31). Thus the motivating and directing energy of human life for Thomas as for Augustine, but not at all as for Aristotle, is love—natural love elevated by grace so as to participate in the very love by which God loves the world.

His teaching, graced by God, made Thomas a saint. His teaching is holy, I have been urging, because it is rooted in the source of all holiness and ever returns to it. With the help of Saint Thomas we can more readily and better obey the injunction of the psalmist when he tells us, "Know that the Lord, Yahweh, He Who Is, is God, He made us, not we ourselves" (Ps 99:3). And we can do that because "there is signed upon us the light of your countenance, Lord" (Ps 4:7).

Chapter Four

Becoming a Great Bookie at Notre Dame

The first secure center, and intellectually the most influential one, I found in the teaching of Saint Thomas Aquinas. But he also in his *Summa theologiae* produced a great book, and the Great Books movement extended the circle of which Thomas remained for me the center.

As I have already noted, I was present at the University of Chicago in 1937 when that movement reached one of the highest points in its development. But at that time, as a mere student, I was only on the edge of that development. It was not until ten years later that I became an active participant in it and entered upon the way that led to my career as a "great bookie". For in 1947 I joined the staff that under the direction of Mortimer Adler was engaged in producing the set published by Encyclopaedia Britannica, Inc., as *Great Books of the Western World*.

If there is any single person who deserves the title of "The Great Bookie", it is certainly Mortimer Adler. He makes no claim to be the originator of the movement. Credit for that he attributes to his own teacher, John Erskine, musician, first president of the Julliard School of Music, novelist, literary critic, and professor of English, who in 1919 inaugurated at Columbia University the Honors Colloquium in the Classics of the Western World. Adler, however, does claim credit for coining the phrase "great books" when he persuaded Hutchins to set up a "great books course" at the University of Chicago, of which I was later a member, as I have already noted.

In 1947 as a member of Adler's staff producing the set of great books, I began as an indexer. My first assignment was to index Plato's *Laws,* Locke's *Second Treatise on Government,* and *The Federalist Papers* by providing references from those books having something to say on the lists of topics that Adler and his first assistant, William Gorman, had drawn up for the indexing staff and that is published as an integral part of the *Syntopicon* volume. In the set as it was finally published, there are some 2,987 topics arranged under 102 ideas, running from ANGEL to WORLD. The idea GOD, for example, which collected the largest number of references from the set, is broken down into seventy-three topics, and under each of these (with the exception of those that are empty headings) references are cited to passages that address them in the 443 works by seventy-one authors included in the published set. Because of this organization the title of the two volumes comprising the elaborate and extensive analytical index is *The Great Ideas: A Syntopicon of Great Books of the Western World,* and constitutes volumes 2 and 3 of the published set of great books.

For each of the 102 ideas, Adler wrote an essay introducing the reader to the discussion of the idea and its topics to be found in the books of the set. He had written about half of the total before he found the format and style that he wanted to follow. This consisted in allowing the authors of the books to speak for themselves, and this entailed revising the essays already written to accomplish this purpose. The production schedule did not allow time for Adler to make this revision himself, since he still had the rest of the essays to write. Hence my second task was to take the essays that Adler had already written and supply the words of the great book authors whose positions were being discussed.

My final contribution to the production of the *Syntopicon* was the general review that I and three other editors made of every reference cited under every topic. One week a month for almost two years we met with Adler to discuss our findings and conclusions about the quality of the referencing and what we had done by deleting and adding to improve it. In all there were about 163,000 references to be checked, and although these were divided among four editors, each of us still had a great many references to review. Such a task could be accomplished only by meeting a very tight schedule of checking so many references each day. The completion of that work marked among other things a triumph of scheduling. The only other scheduling task of comparable magnitude came almost thirty years later when I had to read every article contained in the "Macropaedia" part of the new edition of the *Encyclopaedia Britannica*.

No reasonable person could accept and believe to be true many of the propositions asserted by the authors included in our set of great books, especially those in science and philosophy. For many of them flatly contradicted one another. The books included in the set were selected for a variety of reasons, partly because of the diverse interests and preferences of the board of selection. That there is so much of ancient mathematics—Euclid,

Archimedes, Apollonius, Nicomachus, Ptolemy—probably owes much to the persuasiveness of Buchanan. Aristotle and Aquinas were favorites of Adler, while *Tristram Shandy* was a favorite of Hutchins. The mathematicians just cited are needed for understanding Ptolemy, whose work was read by Copernicus, and then they in turn were taken up by Kepler, Galileo, and Newton. All together compose a wonderful, awe-inspiring story, one that has contributed greatly to the understanding of our intellectual world. But it is also one that is tremendously difficult to read and understand.

Much easier reading, and also much more dubious to my mind, are the works of Marx and Freud. They are more full of error than of truth. Yet without their work how much of twentieth century thought and practice would be impossible to comprehend! Then too as an aid to understanding even the reading of error can be rewarding. Even though they stand in need of correcting, both Marx and Freud have opened up new fields of investigation and new ways of investigating them—Marx of capital, Freud of sexuality and the unconscious.

Yet the greatness of a book lies not only in the great influence that it has exerted but also, and mainly, in the consideration it has given to a great idea such as to reward reading and rereading with continuing illumination and understanding.

Founding a Great Books Program

As my work on the *Syntopicon* was drawing to an end, events were occurring at the University of Notre Dame that were to result in my continuing to work with great books, although in still another way. This development was one in which Adler was again a major mover. The other person who was even more responsible was Fr. John J. Cavanaugh, C.S.C., president of the university from 1946 to 1952.

The material and underlying condition for a change lay in the new situation in which Notre Dame found itself at the end of the war. Before 1941 it is not inaccurate to say that Notre Dame provided a good example of what has come to be called the "Catholic ghetto complex" in that it was a place where Catholic students could withdraw into a totally Catholic environment and learn, treasure, and defend the truths and values of Catholicism. That descriptive name is now usually used in a pejorative sense. But it has become clear following upon the destruction of that "ghetto" after the Second Vatican Council that there was much good in it that has since been lost. A pluralistic society contains many different and diverse goods, but it lacks the special good and beauty of a unitary society founded on deeply shared beliefs.

The war brought with it the establishment of a Naval V-12 training program at Notre Dame, and this opened up the "ghetto" in the university by suddenly introducing much of America's pluralism. As a result of that experience Notre Dame at the end of the war faced a difficult and crucial decision. Would the university try to return to its pre-1941 status and remain fairly small and compact, or would it keep open its doors and be willing to expand and experiment? Father Cavanaugh was as responsible as anyone else, I believe, for the decision to follow the latter way.

That an experiment in a new kind of liberal education

would move in the direction of great books was even more exclusively the initiative of Father Cavanaugh. In the early days of the Great Books movement in adult education, Father Cavanaugh had become an avid "great bookie" and a friend of Adler. He also became closely associated with Roger J. Kiley, judge of the Illinois appellate court in Chicago, an alumnus of Notre Dame, a football great under Rockne and a teammate of "the Gipper", and in the 1940s a member of the "fat men's class" in great books that Adler and Hutchins had in Chicago. In 1945, Kiley began to come to Notre Dame regularly to lead with Father Cavanaugh and Dean Clarence Manion a great books class with a select group of law students.

In the Arts College there was also a small group of faculty members working to introduce the Great Books approach to their teaching. This group included Rufus Rauch and Frank O'Malley of the English department, the former of whom spent a year in the Saint John's program in Annapolis, and Father Thomas J. Brennan, C.S.C., of the philosophy department, who also led a great books adult class in South Bend; and Willis Nutting of the history department.

Father Cavanaugh became president of the university in 1946 and soon began preparing for the introduction of a Great Books program. Toward that end in 1947 he invited Adler to come to Notre Dame for a series of discussions with its faculty on how a Great Books program might be adapted to a Catholic college. By the fall of 1949 the situation was favorable enough to make it feasible to put on a series of great books seminars to demonstrate to the faculty that they should be adopted by Notre Dame. The students for these demonstrations came from a third year philosophy course taught by Father T. J. Brennan, himself a leader in an adult great books seminar. Adler and the four other editors of the *Syntopicon* were to be the principal leaders. Adler himself took the opening seminar on November 4, 1949, for a discussion of the *Oedipus Rex* and *Antigone* of Sophocles. I took the second a week later on the *Meno* of Plato. We met in a large room of the old administration building under the golden dome. The students and their two leaders sat around a large table placed in the center of the room while the attending members of the faculty sat and observed from chairs placed around the walls of the room.

For Father Cavanaugh these seminars marked the end of preparing the ground. By January of 1950 he initiated the establishment of a Great Books program in the Arts College. He could have established such a program by presidential fiat, but he preferred to have the approval of the faculty. As a first step I was called back that same month to discuss with the college faculty what such a program would look like if it were to take all of its students' time for all four undergraduate years. Shortly thereafter I was made director of the General Program of Liberal Studies that opened the fall semester of 1950 with five faculty members and fifty students, which in effect established a college-within-a-college. Father Cavanaugh was optimistic enough to hope that it would prove so successful as to absorb and take over the entire liberal arts college. I was never as sanguine.

Oddly enough, some of the strongest opposition to the introduction of such a program came from friends and colleagues of mine at the Mediaeval Institute in Toronto. The president of the Institute at the time was

Professor Anton Pegis, and he had just published an attack on a Great Books program under the title "Truth and the Great Books".[1] The article seemed to me to pose a threat that I had to meet. I countered its arguments in a five-and-one-half page, single-spaced typed letter that I sent to Father Cavanaugh and that he in turn had copied and distributed among the Notre Dame College faculty. The charges that were made so many years ago against the great books as basic instruments of teaching and learning still remain with us, and for that reason they deserve consideration at some length. But to understand those charges one must know something of the distinctive features of a great books discussion seminar, since it is the seminar that is the principal object of attack.

Such a seminar consists of a rapid reading of a great book followed by a discussion of it with fellow students (at most twenty) and two leaders. The books represent all basic disciplines and are read more or less in the chronological order of their appearance—the great books being those of our Western tradition. The idea of such a seminar was the invention of John Erskine, and he invented it, Adler claims, to provide undergraduates with a college equivalent of the research seminar enjoyed by graduate students,[2] such as I had with Gilson. But instead of a research paper written by a student that is then the subject for discussion, there is the text of a book to be read and discussed under the leadership of a teacher who would function mainly as a better reader.

---

[1] Anton C. Pegis, "Truth and the Great Books", in *Books on Trial,* October–November 1949.

[2] M. J. Adler, *Philosopher at Large* (New York: Macmillan, 1977), 30–31.

Incidentally, when I introduced such a course at Notre Dame and called it a "seminar", the head of the history department at the time, who was himself a research specialist, called me to task for daring to misuse the name of "seminar" for such a vastly different thing from that which had been so called by its inventor, the great German historian, Ranke.

With this much understanding of a great books seminar, we can now turn to the charges that Pegis leveled against it. They reduce to three principal accusations, as follows: (1) a superficial reading of books in many different subject matters, written in many different historical periods, results in "a cruel disfigurement of the great books, of man himself, and of truth", since it constitutes "a skillful exercise in opinion, having neither the health of truth, nor the illness of error"; (2) since the authors of great books were very much men of their own time, their books "must be read with historical fidelity to be understood"; and (3) from these two charges it follows that the books must be read by, or at least under the direction of, a specialist who has been trained to place, understand, and evaluate the book under discussion.[3]

Each of these three charges manifests a complete misconception of the function and purpose of a great books seminar. They also indicate why a person with highly expert understanding of a given book may be a very poor leader of the discussion. He will not want to lead the students in discussion by raising discussable questions; he will want to teach them, to provide a lecture showing his own understanding of the book. No doubt his understanding of the book will be far superior to

---

[3] Pegis, "Truth".

that of the students, who have read the book hurriedly for the first time. The object of the discussion, however, is not so much the book as what the book is about and to encourage and lead the students to discuss that subject and strengthen their own thinking about it. Misreadings should be challenged, especially by the students themselves. Thus the reading and discussion of the *Republic* of Plato can provide an introduction to thinking about the idea of justice and about the many problems that can arise with regard to that idea. Nor is there any reason why the truth of the positions that Plato advocates should not come up for discussion. In fact, the reading of Aristotle's *Politics* will compel in several cases facing that issue directly.

The second charge, that with regard to historical understanding, is likewise beside the mark. It is not the history of thinking about justice, nor whether the situation of Greece at the time Plato wrote may have influenced his thinking, that is in question. Rather, the question is how to begin to think about justice, and Plato is read to help and further the pursuit of that idea. That the *Republic* can accomplish this purpose provides a most telling sign of its greatness. For what it has to say is not limited to either the time, place, or language in which it was written. It is this feature of transcending time and place that makes certain books not only great but greater than others. They have something to say of importance to readers widely separated in time and place regarding matters of perennial significance just because they address concerns, issues, and ideas central to human life. For this reason Hutchins referred to the great books of the Western tradition as constituting "the great conversation".

While on the subject of history, we should also note that the great books contributed tremendously to the making of our intellectual history and thus to preserving its record in writing. To read them in chronological order is consequently to return to the sources of that tradition and to encounter it in the course of its development. It is to read the Plato known by Aristotle; of Augustine, heir of both Plato and Plotinus; of Thomas, the reader of Aristotle and Augustine, all of whom provide living sources for the thought of Gilson and Maritain. Another course, one in imaginative literature, runs from Homer through Virgil down to Dante, then onto Milton, to appear still in the writing of Pound, Eliot, and Joyce. Then too there is the great course in mathematics and science that has already been mentioned.

More recent criticism of the great books of the West compounds the same mistake by also seriously misunderstanding the Western tradition itself. The mistake consists in the claim that all books, and especially great books, are culturally determined by the culture in which they originate. Great books of the Western world are great only in the West where they originated according to this charge. Yet among civilizations and cultures the West is unique in the extent to which its intellectual achievements are transcultural and transcend their own cultures to reach out to people of any culture.

The failure to recognize this fact about the West's intellectual achievements derives from extreme shortsightedness and narrowness of vision; namely, from the failure to distinguish among the different kinds of intellectual endeavor and achievement. The works of science, mathematics, and logic—and the writings in which they are recorded—are entirely transcultural, and people of all cultures come to study them not because they are Western, but because they are true and provide the knowledge needed to produce the wonders of technology.

Works in philosophy, especially in morals and politics, are somewhat more bound to the culture of their origin, but by no means entirely so. Although different beliefs and practices affect one's judgments concerning the good to be achieved, cultural relativity in such matters is not complete. Here again the contribution of the West is unique in the extent in which it provides the materials for the analysis and understanding of the great ideas concerning the good life.

The reading and judgment of imaginative literature, especially of poetry, is of all intellectual works most bound to its culture. This is so mainly because of its close dependence upon the language in which it is written. It is no accident that the word "literature" is usually taken to refer mainly to such works. Dryden, who was no mean poet or critic, maintained that the *Georgics* of Virgil was the best poem ever written. Yet to a reader who knows no Latin this judgment is hard to understand and appreciate when the poem is read in translation. Yet here again a truly great work of imaginative literature transcends its dependence upon its original language. Regardless of its language, one poem or novel may be better than another. It does so by better realizing and achieving the form in which it is expressed and its conventions. The *Iliad, Aeneid, Divine Comedy, Paradise Lost* are each great achievements of their own language and culture; but more than that, and more importantly, they are supremely great as poetic structures of the epic.

Even in religion and theology, where judgment depends upon faith and looks beyond reason, there still remain objective standards, and these must provide a basis for judgment whenever a claim of truth is put forward that can be compared with and tested by other known truths.

Criticism of great books based upon the relativity of history and culture suffers from a failure to grasp a basic distinction in two different kinds of knowledge and understanding. It is the distinction that Aristotle drew between *paideia* and *epistemé,* a distinction of crucial importance for understanding the task of education at the college level. At the beginning of the treatise on the *Parts of Animals,* Aristotle points out that there are

> two ways in which a person may be competent in respect of any study or investigation: ... he may have either what can rightly be called a scientific knowledge of the subject (*epistemé*); or he may have what is roughly described as an educated person's competence (*paideia*), and therefore be able to judge correctly what parts of an exposition are satisfactory and which are not. That, in fact, is the sort of person we take the man of general education (*paideia*) to be; his education (*paideia*) consists of this. In this case, however, we expect to find in the one individual the ability to judge of almost all subjects, whereas in the other case the ability is confined to some special science.[4]

The Greek word *epistemé* was translated into Latin as *scientia* and thence into English as *science,* whereas *paideia* became in Latin *humanitas* with the sense in En-

---

[4] Aristotle, *De partibus animalium,* I.1, 639a7–11.

glish not of humanity or humaneness, but rather of our "humanities". As the Aristotelian text makes clear, the difference between the two corresponds to that between specialized and general knowledge. There is also the implication that the humanities are not to be identified with any particular subject matter and hence also not with any academic department. There is also the further implication, because of the root meaning of the Latin word, that this is the kind of knowledge that makes not the scientist or specialist, but the fully human person.

With this distinction we can at once counter and turn aside the main thrust of the charges made against an education based upon the reading and discussion of great books. Such an education aims at *paideia* and not at *epistemé*, and it is the primary task of the liberal college to place the capstone upon *paideia* that had been begun at the level of elementary and secondary schooling.

The crucial distinction is not between truth and opinion, as Pegis has it, but between *epistemé* and *paideia*. Yet the question of truth is obviously of importance in considering the great books. If by commitment we understand teaching, learning, and holding one definite philosophy and theology, the claim that the great books lack any commitment to the truth contains much truth. It is certainly true that the intellectual tradition of our great books set constitutes a pluralistic society. The unity that it possesses consists not in agreement upon any doctrine claiming to be true but in agreement upon the questions and issues that pose the most significant and important problems and upon which there has been continual thinking, writing, and discussion. The pluralism and disagreement to be found in the great books are so great that it would be possible to use them as a basis for a program of philosophical scepticism.

However, there is no such thing as a single agreed upon program of education based upon the great books. They could be used to form the basis of many different programs as different from one another as the philosophical positions to be found among the great books. Hence too, they could be used as the basis for an educational program with a very definite commitment to the truth. That is what the University of Notre Dame set out to do in 1950 when it established the General Program of Liberal Studies, and it is to describe that program in some detail that I now turn.

Notre Dame's General Program

First, a word about commitment. Ours was intended and organized to be a program professing and practicing the faith of the Roman Catholic Church. That in itself, of course, counts as one very large commitment. But we went still further. For although there are admittedly several different, even competing, Christian philosophies and theologies within the Church, we further committed ourselves to the philosophy and theology of Saint Thomas Aquinas. That commitment was stated clearly and made the basis for the courses, or tutorials, as they were called, devoted to the systematic study of these two disciplines. For this purpose two hours a week were allotted for each discipline for all four years. The method in each was the same and consisted of the intensive reading and analysis of a basic text chosen as providing the best way to the truth upon its subject.

In philosophy we would begin by reading an appropriate dialogue of Plato as providing an introduction and then turn to a text of Aristotle read according to the commentary of Thomas upon it. During the four years, the major parts of philosophy were studied: the philosophy of nature the first year, followed in the second by metaphysics; the philosophy of man was the object of the third year tutorial with the study of philosophical psychology and ethics; the fourth year focused upon social and political philosophy and intensive study was also made of *The Federalist Papers*.

In theology the first year was devoted to the study of Sacred Scripture, and the following three years to that of systematic theology. Here the basic texts were those of Saint Augustine, Saint Thomas, and conciliar and papal pronouncements. Reason and revelation, and the divine essence and trinity were considered in the second year; creation, redemption, and the virtues in the third; and in the fourth, sacrifice, sacraments, the mystical body, and the social teaching of the Church.

As is evident from even so brief a description, the tutorials in philosophy and theology were definitely "committed". However, I should also note that these two series of tutorials by no means exhausted the reading in philosophy and theology. Indeed, much more reading in these disciplines was done in the great books seminars, which included modern as well as ancient and mediaeval books. Also in the language tutorials, especially during the first two years, shorter texts from both disciplines were read for comparison with other kinds of writing.

At the time the program began in 1950 the most innovative part of it, aside from the great dependence upon great books and the seminar discussion, was undoubtedly the language tutorial. This met five periods a week throughout the year. It combined features of both the seminar and the tutorials in philosophy and theology. Like the tutorials, it was intensive in purpose in that it consisted of an intensive reading of a few selected texts. Unlike them, however, and like the seminar, it did not confine itself to any one subject matter or discipline. Its aim was training in the basic Trivium: grammar, rhetoric, and logic. For this purpose texts were chosen from different subject matters that represented not only different ways of knowing, but also different ways of writing. Texts were usually selected from books also read in seminar, but only a few passages from a few books.

In 1950 students entering Notre Dame had usually studied Latin for at least two years. Thus after a review of Latin based on a study of the Ordinary of the Mass, the language tutorial I conducted read the following texts:

Gospel of Saint John, prologue
Saint Thomas: *De verbo, Summa theologiae,* I.34.1–3
Genesis: The Joseph story
Lucretius: *De natura rerum,* III. 1024–94
Virgil: *Georgics,* II. 458–540
Virgil: *Aeneid,* I. 450–93
Cicero: *De officiis,* I.iv–v
Tacitus: *Annals,* III. 26–28; VI. 23–25
Saint Augustine: *Confessions,* IX. 23–25

Although the texts were read in Latin, the aim was not to attempt to make Latinists out of the students. Its purpose was to use the Latin along with English to develop skill and understanding in the basic arts of language.

The second year of the language tutorial was like

the first, but with French instead of Latin. The third year was devoted to the theory and practice of literary criticism, and the fourth to the study of tragedy and the novel.

The tutorial in mathematics and science was organized so as to study in the first year Euclid's geometry and some elementary conic sections from Apollonius, and to turn in the second year to the analytical geometry of Descartes and an introduction to calculus. Experimental science was the object of the third year's study of science, and biological science was studied the fourth year.

As originally established, the program aimed to secure and assure an integrated intellectual community, something that no contemporary university is. The principal means was to develop an omnicompetent faculty in the sense that every member would be expected to know, as teacher or student, every course that its students were required to study. This ideal was never realized, except for the seminars, which all of the faculty would eventually come to know through actually having to teach them.

As director, partly by way of example and more so from my own personal interest, I can say that I believe without exaggeration that I did more than anyone else on the faculty to realize that ideal. At the risk of betraying the sin of vainglory, I will list by title the courses that I taught during my years of teaching in the program.

> Latin and the Arts of the Trivium
> French and the Arts of the Trivium
> Euclid's *Elements*
> Descartes's *Geometry*
> Plato's *Timaeus* and Aristotle's *Physics*

Russell and Whitehead: *Principia mathematica* I
Mathematical Logic, especially syllogistic
Methods of Knowing
Kant's Philosophy of Science
Intellectual History
Philosophical Inquiry
Origins of Christianity
Concepts of Man
Metaphysics
Great books seminars throughout

Such great diversity, one may say, cannot help but make for superficiality. And if such a course of study makes for the generalist, where does it leave the specialist? This question raises one of the greatest difficulties and the most acute source of strain for a faculty member in a program such as the one I have been describing. It obviously attracts those who are devoted to a life of learning. But as one's learning grows and develops it soon wants to venture into areas and pursue directions that lie beyond the needs and wishes of an undergraduate college student. The tension mounts between the needs of teaching and the desire for research. That may be faced by any undergraduate teacher. But it is more intense in a Great Books program, which unlike other departments in a comprehensive university has no graduate extension that can serve as an outlet for such yearnings and ambitions. To add to the frustration it is usually through just such outlets that advancement in the academic profession can be obtained. Often a faculty member becomes so dissatisfied that he will seek a way out by locating a slot in a department that possesses a graduate program as well as a "major concentration".

The program at Notre Dame enjoyed a distinct advantage in that, as a college-within-a-college, it is surrounded by research and graduate programs in the other departments. Thus it has been possible for a faculty member of the General Program to offer occasionally graduate courses in other departments. Thus members have taken advantage of this opportunity to offer courses in the philosophy, history, and English departments. Frequently too this experience has resulted in the production of research papers, unfortunately necessary for advancement in this day of "publish or perish".

However, there is a special and particularly important benefit that a Great Books program derives from being a part of a Catholic university. As Cardinal Newman noted in his defense of the university, wherever a commitment to theology is lacking there will be a hole, an emptiness, which has to be filled, and if it is not filled by theology some other discipline inevitably will endeavor to take its place.[5] Devotion to the great books divorced from a theological and religious commitment all too readily moves over to fill that empty place and to become a quasi religion. The most ostensive sign of such devotion that I know of is the temple to the great books that Wabash College has erected in its new library. I suspect that it was probably built at the behest of a donor who was a great bookie and made that room a condition of his gift. It is a splendid large room, walled in marble, with the names of the authors of the great books carved as a frieze around the top of the walls. It has the appearance and feel of a temple, but, if so, it is a temple to a false god.

---

[5] John Henry Cardinal Newman, *The Idea of a University* (New York; Holt, Rinehart, and Winston, 1966), 55.

The great books that made and recorded our intellectual tradition cannot and should not be more than a means to develop our minds through deepening our understanding along the road that we are hopefully traveling to that wisdom that lies in the worship of the one and only true God. As Saint Thomas once wrote: "Although it is not in our power to know by ourselves the things of faith, nevertheless, if we do what we can, that is to say, if we follow the guidance of natural reason, God will not fail to give us what is necessary to us."[6]

The Program, 1950–63

When established in 1950, the General Program called for all four years of its students' career for all required courses, without any electives. However, only four classes were graduated that pursued the complete four-year program. The change came in 1952, when Father Theodore Hesburgh became president of the university. For in that year a common freshman year, which went into effect in 1957, was set up for all incoming students. With this innovation the Great Books program not only lost a year, but some of its own requirements were met during the first year. These included requirements in foreign language, mathematics, and laboratory science. Such changes necessitated a wholesale reorganization of the General Program. Rather than attempting to provide a detailed review of the various changes, I will summarize them by describing the shape the program came to have by 1963–64, which was the last year that I was its director.

[6] Thomas Aquinas, *De veritate*, q.14, a.11, ad 2.

The tutorials in language, mathematics, and science were reduced to the following courses: Language and Logic, mainly devoted to mathematical logic in the sophomore year; the History of Science in the junior year; and the Methodology and Philosophy of Science in the senior year. A literature sequence was set up following a genre approach with separate courses devoted to the study of poetry, tragedy, the novel, and literary criticism. Philosophy had three semester courses, as had theology, each of them following much the same order as that already noted for the four-year sequence. The Great Books Seminar remained the same except that it was reduced to a three-year sequence.

Two other innovations should be noted. A lecture course in historical orientation was introduced as a small means of overcoming the students' appalling ignorance of chronological development; their inability was so great that often they could not place even within centuries the time at which a book was written. Another reduction came from the felt and expressed need of the students for time to take at least one elective course a semester during the last two years.

After these changes the General Program became much less distinctive than it had been at its beginning. Much that was good was undoubtedly lost. It no longer enjoyed the strong sense of community that it had possessed as a college-within-a-college. Yet some of the reductions had distinct advantages. It was a relief, at least administratively, not to be burdened with the task of trying to locate scientists who would be willing and able to teach the laboratory sciences within the context of the great books. Instead, the program could turn its interest to the history and philosophy of science. In fact, one of the earliest graduates from the program, Michael Crowe, obtained a doctoral degree in the history of science and returned to offer the first course in it at Notre Dame.

The foreign language requirement became a responsibility of the common freshman year. This, along with the possibility of taking elective courses, enabled students to increase their proficiency in a foreign language. This possibility became increasingly desirable with the introduction of the "year-abroad" programs. The electives also provided the students with an opportunity to obtain a "major concentration" in a particular discipline, especially if it built upon the strong foundation in literature and philosophy within the program.

The General Program, now known as the Program of Liberal Studies, remains distinctly different from other programs at Notre Dame. It still forms an intellectual community from its commitment to learning and teaching the great books. The seminar thus remains the center on which that community is based, since it is shared by students and faculty alike, however different their special interests may be.

I went on an extended leave from Notre Dame in 1964, and although I returned in 1970, I never thereafter had much to say about the direction of the General Program.

During my years at Notre Dame, from which I retired in 1977, all but two were under the presidency of Father Hesburgh, who remained a strong supporter of the Great Books program. During that period the university almost quadrupled the size of its student body, its faculty, and its buildings. It admitted women students and faculty members. It increased its graduate school, with corresponding emphasis upon scholarship and teaching, and this is almost certain to result in the deteriorization of its undergraduate teaching. It became "secularized" as it would never have dreamed of becoming when I entered in 1950.

Is Notre Dame today a better university than it was in 1950? Measured by the secular standards of non-Catholic universities, there is no doubt that it is. Its faculty is more scholarly and scientific. It has more publication and research to its credit. Its students score higher on the entrance tests. It is more international.

Yet it certainly is not as manifestly Catholic as it was. But then, of course, neither is the Church in the United States. Now neither the faculty nor the students, I believe, practice their faith as regularly as they did then, even though there may be more interest in religion and theology as an intellectual subject. It is less Catholic in that it no longer supports the universal, that is, the "catholic" mission of the Church under the leadership of the pope as strongly as it once did. The Magisterium of the Church under its head seems almost to be forgotten as a teacher. Latin, the official language of the Church, is all but forgotten, even among seminarians.

The changes in the religious character of the university derive, mostly, it seems to me, from the policy that has been adopted for the hiring of faculty. The administration now hires for its faculty many men and women who are not Catholic and who have no interest in or intent of promoting the truths and values of the Catholic Church.

In the 1950s I was a member of the Faculty Hiring Committee, a body appointed by the administration to put pressure upon the department heads to seek for and hire the best candidates they could find for positions that became open. As it turned out, I became the one member of the committee who asked the candidate, when he was not a Catholic, about his ability and willingness to live and function in a Catholic university. Usually, of course, he foresaw no difficulty, since if he had any such doubts he probably would not have applied for the position in the first place. The committee functioned as a kind of watch force to encourage departments to improve the qualities of their faculty and so too the excellence of the university. Father Cavanaugh was looking to that same end when he started the General Program.

The times have brought great changes to the campus in still other ways. At its inception in 1950 the Great Books program was the most "liberal" one in the university. It assigned books that were on the Index of Prohibited Books, for which permission had to be obtained from the president. Discussion seminars were held in which the students were encouraged to speak out and not just listen to their professors. The texts for study were great and difficult books, not just hashed down versions of them. All of this has now become standard practice throughout the university. But the Great Books program is also now considered one of the most "conservative" and reputedly the most Catholic.

I do not think that the program today is as good as it was in its first years. In theology and philosophy it has been watered down so that it no longer studies as intensively and extensively as it once did the writings of Plato and Aristotle, Saint Augustine and Saint Thomas. It has opened its readings to classics of the Orient, thereby further diluting its study of the Western tradition. There is also less study of logic and mathematics than there used to be and so less in the way of discipline and rigor. More attention is given to the fine arts. As a whole, the program is less "intellectualistic" than it was in the beginning. Yet it remains a program that is highly intellectual in that it places its work upon the primacy of the intellect in education. So although less so than it once was, in this respect it still remains faithful to the teaching of Saint Thomas Aquinas.

Chapter Five

Making Sense of Philosophy

The study of philosophy can be wearisome and frustrating, especially if one tries to consider the whole of it in its historical development from the Pre-Socratics to the Post-Wittgensteinians. Some thinkers have found it so difficult that they think it is a hopeless task to try to make sense of it and that the best thing to do is to start anew. I do not find that such a radically despairing position was ever taken in either the time of ancient or of mediaeval philosophy. Some thinkers may have abandoned philosophy as a lost and hopeless cause. But Aristotle was engaged certainly in the same enterprise that Plato was engaged in, and Saint Thomas, theologian that he was, continued to carry on from Saint Augustine with the help of Aristotle. It seems that it is only in our own modern era that philosophers have thought it incumbent upon them to dump the whole enterprise as it was practiced before they came along. Descartes refused to place any trust in sense experience and, relying on ideas alone, repudiated the philosophical thought of the past as based on that fallacious trust. Kant, on the other hand, exulting in the triumph of Newton's physics in its account of the phenomenal world, repudiated any reason that claimed to go beyond the reach of the experience of sense. Wittgenstein, bemused by the way that language can mislead thought, repudiated much of the philosophical endeavor as founded upon mistakes that language had inflated into imaginary problems. The result of all three of these "revolutions" in philosophy resulted in its impoverishment. If one followed Descartes, there was little to be learned from continuing to read the writings of the ancient and mediaeval thinkers. If Kant was your master, there also ceased to be little excuse for continuing to study Descartes and his followers. And if you were a Wittgensteinian, there was no longer any need to read any of the previous philosophers, except to show how they had become so caught in the snares of language as to be unable to identify a genuine philosophical problem.

Making sense of philosophy and its history is not easy. The attempt pursued by the "revolutionaries" just mentioned also has not succeeded. Each has attracted followers, who have contributed to developing a certain line of thought that has produced a few results. But none of them has succeeded in its first purpose, which was the destruction of all philosophy previous to the individual's attempted revolution. The philosophers from the Pre-Socratics on continue to be read and to be read profitably, as Heidegger offers a preeminent witness of the value of the earliest.

However, the usual way of attempting to make sense of philosophy has been of little help. Why should one go from the Pre-Socratics to Plato and on to Aristotle, the Stoics, Plotinus and the Neo-Platonists, from the Fathers of the Church to the Scholastics, from Descartes through Locke, Berkeley, and Hume, to Kant, Hegel onto Heidegger, and from then onto Wittgenstein?

Some sense has been made of that long and large development. But for the most part that has consisted in identifying among the mass of writings certain schools of thought: followers of Plato became Platonists, and in the same way others became Aristotelians, Augustinians, Cartesians, Kantians, Hegelians, Wittgensteinians, and so on. This move provided a little help toward understanding because it did succeed in identifying a number of philosophers who agreed with one another on their inspiration and on their basic principles. However, this much did little to tell why one group of thinkers disagreed with the others. It failed to explain the relation between the various families of thinkers.

Suppose we grant that the history of philosophy, at least in the West, is a mess, a mass of disagreements and even of contradictions. What are we going to do about it? I have been fortunate to have known and to have been a student of two thinkers who have addressed this very problem, and who have proposed and practiced two different ways of making sense of this confusion. I have already mentioned both of them and even paid some tribute to them, and more tribute is still to come. One is Etienne Gilson, the other Mortimer Adler. I mention both of them here for two reasons. First, because I have learned from them how to make sense of philosophy. Second, because I have attempted to put into practice in my own research and writing the methods of each, although more of Adler's, because I have been more closely associated with him. Hence I will have more to say here of my application of the Adlerian way of making sense of philosophy.

Gilson's Way

At the start we must distinguish between two Gilsons: one, the historian who expounds and interprets the thought of, especially, mediaeval thinkers; the other, the philosopher who seeks to make sense of philosophical history and development. The first one writes as a historian, the second as a philosopher but as one who makes a special use of history.

We must also take into account the fact that there are several different ways of making sense of philosophy. The simplest is to make sense of the thought of a single philosopher, which is a task that requires unusual ability. The difficulty is greatest for those writers who lived in a past remote from ours and worked in a context that is foreign to us in many ways. In this kind of analysis and exposition Gilson excelled, as is evident from his masterful accounts of the thought of Saint Augustine, Saint Bonaventure, Saint Thomas Aquinas, and Duns Scotus. Such an understanding, however, makes sense not of philosophy as such but only of the philosophy of one writer.

A great thinker and writer who also influences many others attracts followers and in effect establishes a family. It consists of his followers who develop his own thought while adhering to his basic principles. To identify such families makes still further sense of philosophy by comprehending the thought of many men in addition to that of the founding father of the family. Gilson was especially talented in diagnosing the features that serve to identify a philosophical or theological family. His history of mediaeval thought so distinguishes many different families. As an example of his method, herewith are the characteristic traits that typify the Augustinian family of thinkers:

[1] There is no Augustinism without the fundamental postulate that true philosophy implies an act of adherence

Making Sense of Philosophy

to the supernatural order which frees the will from the flesh through grace and the mind from scepticism through revelation.

[2] Digression is Augustinism's natural method. The natural order of an Augustinian doctrine is to branch out around one center, and this is precisely the order of charity.

[3] The more a doctrine tends to be built around charity the more Augustinian it is.

[4] When there are two equally possible solutions to one and the same problem, an Augustinian doctrine will incline spontaneously towards that which concedes less to nature and more to God.

[5] The Christian philosopher considers revelation a source of light for his reason.

[6] The certainty with which the soul apprehends itself is the first of all certitudes and the criterion of truth.

[7] The soul is better known than the body.

[8] The path leading to God must of necessity pass through the mind because God is better known to us than the body.[1]

Such being the traits of the Augustinian family of thinkers, Gilson claims that they characterize a "doctrine whose spirit and fundamental positions . . . has already had a career extending over fifteen centuries, and there is no indication as to when it will end".[2] Among the members of this family sharing a common inspiration, he includes Saint Anselm, Saint Bonaventure, and Malebranche.

---

[1] Etienne Gilson, *The Christian Philosophy of Saint Augustine*, trans. L. E. M. Lynch (New York: Random House, 1960), 235–43.
[2] Ibid.

To interpret the history of philosophy in this way makes more sense of philosophy than the interpretation of one philosopher does. It not only furthers understanding by extending it to many other thinkers, but also by being able to shed sudden light outside its own family. It can show, for example, that Descartes is a remote relative of the Augustinian family. However, this method fails to confront the great scandal: the radical disagreement between philosophers and their families who hold different and even contradictory positions. For this a method is needed that is more philosophical and not as bound to history as that of understanding philosophy through coming to know its families.

Gilson himself recognized this need and set out to meet it. He provided such a method principally in two books: *The Unity of Philosophical Experience* and *Being and Some Philosophers*. As he stated expressly in the latter book, but the same applies to the former, "this is not a book in the history of philosophy; it is a philosophical book, and a dogmatically philosophical one at that."[3] Each of these two books has a thesis to proclaim and to expound. The first is that the attempt to replace traditional metaphysics of the science of being qua being by some other science leads to the destruction of philosophy as well as that of metaphysics. The second is that the attempt to erect a metaphysics as a science of being qua being by leaving out existence leads to disaster and again to the destruction of metaphysics.

Before considering the result that Gilson reached, we need to look further at the distinction that he drew

---

[3] Etienne Gilson, *Being and Some Philosophers* (Toronto: Pontifical Institute of Mediaeval Studies, 1952), ix–x.

Making Sense of Philosophy

between the books of his that were historical and those that were philosophical. For it is with respect to this distinction that Adler parts company with him in the way of making sense of philosophy.

Gilson noted that the way that distinguished the work he did as history from that that he did as philosophy was based on the element of choice. As he wrote,

> the only task of history is to understand and to make understood, whereas philosophy must choose; and applying to history for reasons to make a choice is no longer history, it is philosophy. . . . Its object has neither past nor future, for it *is,* that is it is *being,* and the truth about it cannot be proved, it can only be seen—or overlooked. . . . Any approach to truth is bound to be a personal one.[4]

This is a rich and telling passage and, for me, a discouraging one. For in one respect it amounts to admitting that the best way to make sense of all the disagreements of philosophers finally consists in making a personal choice and so, in my case, of accepting and making my own Gilson's personal way of making sense of philosophy. Yet there is a way out of this difficulty. There is an ambiguity, if not a contradiction, in the position that Gilson takes here; and it concerns the truth. Gilson, in his academic world, chose to be known as a historian and not as a philosopher. Why? Because historians are seeking to find out the truth of what has happened, whereas philosophers, as he knew them, are not. But then when he seeks to find the truth among the contentions of philosophers and sets out his findings, what is

[4] Ibid.

the conclusion that he finally reaches? It all remains up to the personal choice of the philosopher.

Now that as a conclusion of his philosophical investigations I do not see as following, nor do I believe that Gilson himself accepted it. I am convinced that he truly believed that he had discovered truths about modern philosophy. Adler agreed with him about these matters. And so do I.

Adler's Way

To tell the story in my way as I have come to understand it, let me try to describe the difference that I see between Gilson's and Adler's way of making sense.[5]

At the start let me state clearly and emphatically that I think that Gilson and Adler are in basic agreement about one thing: both agree that modern philosophy from Descartes on has been badly mistaken and should look for correction to ancient and mediaeval philosophy. Gilson, at the conclusion of his philosophical investigation into the exhaustion of modern philosophy, which he wrote in 1937, declared: "I even hope that it will soon cease to be at all. For what is now called philosophy is either collective mental slavery or skepticism."[6] Because of that belief Gilson, at the College de France, preferred to appear a historian rather than as a philosopher. In 1985, some forty-eight years later, Adler wrote a book entitled *Ten Philosophical Mistakes* in which he

---

[5] Most of this analysis of the Adlerian way was previously published as "A Dialectical Version of the Philosophical Discussion", in *Freedom and the Modern World,* ed. M. D. Torre (Notre Dame, Ind.: American Maritain Association, 1989), 57–63.

[6] Gilson, *The Unity,* 294.

castigated modern philosophy for many of the same mistakes that Gilson would also have condemned. As Father Shook has pointed out, Gilson came to agree with the positions that Adler took in his philosophical writings.[7] Yet Gilson took exception to Adler's way of making sense of philosophy, as Adler never did of Gilson's. Why?

Adler's method grew and developed from his long and deep concern with controversy in philosophy. His concern was not so much that, like Kant, he deplored the existence and extent of disagreement in philosophy. It was rather that he thought that the disagreement was not sharp and clear enough, and more often than not that it amounted to little more than non-agreement of minds that never met and so were incapable of giving rise to a genuine controversy. Non-agreement does not constitute disagreement and hence does not generate a genuine controversy. It makes no more than a difference of opinion. Hence Adler, from his very first book in 1927, called for the construction of a *summa dialectica* that would have as its purpose the task of analyzing, mapping and clarifying the controversy regarding basic philosophical ideas.[8]

To carry out this task and accomplish it, the Institute for Philosophical Research was founded in 1952 with a grant from the Ford Foundation. The method of analysis was developed and perfected and put to the work that resulted in the immense two-volume *Idea of Freedom*. This was followed by four shorter books that applied

---

[7] Shook, *Etienne Gilson,* 384.
[8] Mortimer J. Adler, *Dialectic* (London: Kegan, Paul, Trench, Trubner & Co., 1927), 238–42.

the same method of analysis: *The Idea of Happiness,* by V. J. McGill; *The Idea of Love,* by Robert G. Hazo; *The Idea of Progress,* by Charles Van Doren; and my own *The Idea of Justice.* I also wrote a shorter essay on justice, another on the idea of equality, and another on "The Controversy Regarding the Objectivity of Moral Values". The method employed in these books and articles is the one I have been referring to as the Adlerian one of making sense of philosophy. For the description and analysis of that method I will take as an example my own work on the idea of justice. I do so not only because it is there that I know best what is involved, but also because, as Adler wrote in the preface to my book on the subject, "The work that the Institute has done on the ideas of freedom, progress, happiness, and love . . . has not eventuated in the formulation of a controversy that is nearly as well structured as . . . in the case of justice."[9]

Hence as an exemplary case of the method of analysis at work, the idea of justice offers a clearer and simpler instance than any of the other "idea" books. My understanding and application of the method comes from what I have learned of it from Mortimer Adler. With this proviso I will provide now a simplified version of how a genuine controversy can be established where before one did not exist.

First, if there is to be a genuine controversy, there must be real and not merely apparent disagreement. Hence there are certain previous conditions that have to be met. The first of these conditions is that the partici-

---

[9] Otto A. Bird, *The Idea of Justice* (New York: Praeger, 1967), xi.

Making Sense of Philosophy

pants to the controversy must be talking about the same subject and not just about the same word if that word is used to have different references. Nor need that word be the same thing in every case. One person may be speaking of "freedom", whereas another talks of "liberty", and yet both are talking about the same subject. Such a qualification is obvious if the writers are using different languages. The first problem is to have an identifiable subject of discussion that is addressed by all who enter that discussion whatever their language and terminology.

This first requirement must be further qualified so as to be taken in a minimalist sense. It is not necessary that all talking about justice, for example, should understand by that term the same thing in every respect. It is sufficient that there should be one respect in which all participants agree about the subject that they are talking about.

The second requirement for a good controversy is that this one identifiable subject be such that questions raised about it can elicit different answers and so establish different positions with regard to the questions. In short, for a general disagreement to arise there must be first some subject about which questions can be raised and to which different answers can be given.

Thirdly, and most importantly, for the answers and the positions taken to be such as to generate any considerable controversy, they must have some relation to one another and be coordinated into a theory that claims to explain and make understandable the subject and the issues about it.

There are three clarifications that should be made about these three preliminary conditions for genuine controversy. The first is that for real and not merely apparent disagreement to exist there are three initial agreements that have to be accepted: (1) agreement upon the subject under discussion, (2) agreement about the questions that can legitimately be made about that subject, and (3) agreement about what it is that counts as an answer to the questions asked about the subject.

The requirements just listed for a genuine controversy constitute an ideal of what controversy ought to be. However, it must be noted immediately that the actual historical discussion of a great idea rarely observes any of these initial agreements; nor are they even noted or commented upon. Even Aristotle, who began a dialectical analysis of the thought of his predecessors, did so for doctrinal purposes, to distinguish the true from the false in their accounts and to take the true for the development of his own doctrine. Hence for the most part in order to describe, analyze, and clarify a controversy about a basic idea, it is necessary to construct a controversy that ought to have taken place by identifying its basic subject and distinguishing the issues on which genuinely opposed positions have been taken.

The Idea of Justice: An Example

Thus in investigating the idea of justice, the first task consisted in examining the major theories that have been identified as dealing with justice. Considerable time and effort had to be expended in studying those theories in order to determine which of them fulfilled our basic conditions for controversy. This work demanded the writing of many reports analyzing theories of justice from Plato and Aristotle down to the present, all from our special point of view. These studies ultimately made it possible to identify a common subject that many authors would agree in accepting as one that they would recognize as justice. That subject is identified by the notes or characteristics that it is judged to have, which are gathered from a consideration of the kinds of things that the theories would agree upon in calling just. This examination yielded three notes that serve to identify the idea of justice: (1) justice is a social norm, (2) it is approbative, and (3) it is obligatory.

To say that justice in our minimal sense is a social norm is to claim that it is a relational concept that involves many terms, that it is social in that it applies to persons associated with one another, and that it serves as a norm for directing persons in their dealings with one another.

However, more than this one note is needed, since society has more norms than justice alone. There are norms of manners and decency, of taste, of grammar, and of logic, and none of these are matters of justice except in an extended sense. Justice is more closely linked than any of these norms with those of law and morality. Yet neither of these can provide a further note for identifying justice as a common subject of dispute, since disagreement arises about the relation of justice to both law and morality. But that justice is an approbative concept has no such trouble. The theories are in agreement that when one claims that X is just, he is evaluating that X as good and as something that he would approve of. That claim is the expression of a *pro* attitude toward X. Hence it involves also the emotional side of human nature and enters into the world of value.

The third and final note that determines justice as a common subject of discussion is that it is obligatory. It establishes an *ought*. The just thing to do is something that ought to be done; the unjust thing something that ought not be done. This much is not in dispute. Dispute occurs as soon as one inquires into the foundation of that *ought,* and whether that basis is moral and objective or derives from something else.

These three notes determining justice as a common subject have been found in the literature concerning justice, although explicit discussion of each of them is not always present. This discovery is a dialectical one because it concerns how men have thought and written about justice. It may be of some help to a person endeavoring to come to a true understanding of what justice is. However, that is not the reason why we needed these notes. We located and identified them as a means of obtaining a better understanding of the dispute and controversy concerning justice. These notes in establishing a common subject provide the evidence needed to show that the participants in the dispute are indeed talking about the same thing.

The next step in constructing the controversy consisted in identifying questions about the common notes that all writers on the subject address and to which they offer answers, which in some cases may differ and be opposed to one another. Not all questions that arise in the discussion are equally useful for our purpose. Some theories of justice may emphasize special concerns, as Hegel does about freedom or Del Vecchio about spirit, which raise questions that other theories do not consider at all. Such concerns may well illuminate the nature of justice. But they do not aid understanding

Making Sense of Philosophy

of the general controversy, because they are not of common concern and hence not fundamental to it.

The questions that are fundamental to the general controversy are those that formulate issues regarding the common notes; issues on which differing and opposed positions may be taken; answers that taken together constitute a theory that claims to provide an explanation of the identifying notes. For the idea of justice, six questions are sufficient to identify and distinguish the major different theories about it. Each of these questions formulates a distinct issue, as follows:

1. Is justice the same as legality?
2. Is justice a criterion of law?
3. Is justice based on natural right?
4. Is justice, in any other sense than that of legality, an objective norm of human action?
5. Is justice obligatory on its own apart from legal or social sanctions?
6. Is justice a distinct virtue?

In most cases the wording of the issue shows its relation to the common notes. Thus law establishes a norm that is in some sense both approbative and obligatory. Hence the first four questions deal with justice as a norm: whether or not it is to be identified with law, that is, with positive, man-made law; whether or not it provides a criterion of law; whether or not it is based on natural right.

Each of the questions is such as to yield a "yes" or "no" answer and thus provides a dichotomous criterion of classification. Some of the questions are so related that the answer to one question entails an answer to another. Thus, for example, to claim that justice is the same as legality is also to deny that it is a criterion of law and that it is based on natural right. As a result it is possible to obtain different combinations of affirmative and negative answers to the questions. These answers put together serve to identify the basic theories of justice and thus map the controversy of justice as a whole.

The answers to these questions to be found in the literature on justice reveal that there are only three theories of justice that are basic to or paradigmatic of the general controversy.

One theory, and the simplest, answers the first question in the affirmative by claiming that justice is identical with positive law but denies all the remaining five questions. Hence it can be called the Positive Law theory of justice. Hobbes and the contemporary Scandinavian writer Alf Ross are good representatives of this theory.

At the other extreme is the Natural Right theory of justice. This theory answers the first question in the negative by denying that justice is identical with legality and then answers all the remaining five questions in the affirmative. Aristotle and Adler himself are holders of this position.

The third paradigm, the Social Good theory of justice, falls in between these two. It answers the first and third questions in the negative by denying that justice is identical with positive law or is founded on natural rights. It replies in the affirmative to questions 2, 4, and 5 by claiming that justice is a criterion of law, that it is an objective norm of action, and that it is obligatory apart from legal sanctions. It qualifies its affirmative answer to the sixth question by assimilating justice to the virtue of benevolence. Hume and John Stuart Mill are typical representatives of the Social Good theory.

Making Sense of Philosophy

These three theories are paradigmatic of the general controversy concerning justice in that they provide the types according to which any theory of justice can be measured and located. They locate the particular grouping of positions according to which the entire controversy can be viewed. Combinations of any of the three may and do occur. In fact, many of the recent theories, especially those put forward by Anglo-American thinkers, can be understood as efforts to combine the Social Good and the Natural Right theories, notably the highly touted theory advanced by John Rawls.

A Dialectical Solution

The main purpose of making such a construction, for a construction it is, lies in its effort to make sense of the frequently confusing discussions of philosophers. It does so by attempting to find the issues on which there is real and not merely apparent agreement and disagreement and to state these issues in a language that is both clear and neutral with respect to any of the theories that it analyzes. Some philosophers, notably Descartes, Kant, and Wittgenstein, have attributed confusion to the lack of a proper method for solving philosophical problems. Adler's contention in this respect is that there has not been a good controversy because the issues of agreement and disagreement have not been clearly stated. The result: not disagreement, but non-agreement—trains passing in the night.

The method of reading philosophical literature that we have analyzed is one way of making sense of that literature. Its matter is provided by the writings that have been produced during the long history of philosophy. Yet the method and its results are neither philosophical nor historical, neither a philosophical nor a historical account of thinking about justice. Its object as well as its subject has been not the idea of justice itself, but rather the theories and literature about that idea. Philosophical it may be in that it addresses the writings of philosophers; and historical in that they occurred in a historical context. Yet the result that the method obtains is neither philosophical nor historical, but dialectical.

However, to note that this method is dialectical is not particularly illuminating, since dialectic has meant many things in philosophical discussion. Adler, while he was engaged in perfecting the method and putting it to work in the analysis of the idea of freedom, had occasion to write an essay on the subject of dialectic.[10] In this essay he distinguished this kind of dialectic from two other kinds.

One theory of dialectic identifies it with the very method of philosophy and the knowledge that it achieves. This is Noetic dialectic and has Plato as its foremost representative. Another kind of dialectic may be called Regulative because it is taken as the fundamental law underlying the development of both reality and history. This kind of dialectic is best seen in the work of Hegel and Marx. The third kind of dialectic is not identified either with philosophy or with ontological and historical development. It is taken as an auxiliary of philosophy rather than philosophy itself. Hence it may be called the Reflexive theory of dialectic. Of this Aristotle is the earliest and foremost representative.

---

[10] Mortimer J. Adler, *"The Idea of Dialectic"*, in *The Great Ideas Today*, 1986 (Chicago: Encyclopaedia Britannica, 1986), 154–84.

The method that has been applied here to the idea of justice is obviously closer to the Reflexive kind than to either the Noetic or the Regulative. Yet it differs sharply from Aristotle's use of it. He made a dialectical examination of the work of his predecessors, but he did so with a doctrinal and not a dialectical purpose in view. He used the work of his predecessors as a means of advancing his own investigation of things. His writings reveal his use of that method for the further purpose of discovering the truth about reality.

Our use of the Reflexive dialectic does not aim so high. The truth that it seeks is the truth about philosophical discussion and literature, as in that that has been devoted to the ideas of freedom and of justice. Its hope, of course, is that it may offer help to further the philosophical search for the truth about the ideas with which it deals.

Two Ways: Gilson's and Adler's

The analysis of the controversy concerning justice shows how the Adlerian way makes sense of philosophy. It aims to provide a clarification by locating the major issues on which there is agreement and disagreement and relating the positions taken upon them that together constitute the places of controversy. The result is a map that, while simplified, sketches the main lines of the discussion.

Gilson's way of making sense is obviously very different. Consider the conclusions that he reached in *The Unity of Philosophical Experience*. As is manifested in this title, he claimed to have found and demonstrated a unity, and not as we did the main lines of a controversy.

He did so by using the history of philosophy as a laboratory in which to carry out and test an experiment, namely: What happens to philosophy when some other knowledge than metaphysics is put in its place? After analyzing the mathematicism, spiritualism, and idealism that Descartes spawned and begot, the physicism of Kant, and the socialism of Comte, Gilson concluded with a philosophical moral that he expressed in seven laws:

[1] Philosophy always buries its undertakers.

[2] By his very nature, man is a metaphysical animal.

[3] Metaphysics is the knowledge gathered by a naturally transcendent reason in its search for first principles, or first causes, of what is given in sensible experience.

[4] As metaphysics aims at transcending all particular knowledge, no particular science is competent either to solve metaphysical problems, or to judge their metaphysical solutions.

[5] The failures of the metaphysicians flow from their unguarded use of a principle of unity present in the human mind.

[6] Since being is the first principle of all human knowledge, it is a fortiori the first principle of metaphysics.

[7] All the failures of metaphysics should be traced to the fact that the first principle of human knowledge has been either overlooked or misused by the metaphysicians.[11]

From the two very different kinds of conclusions that the methods obtain it is clear that the Gilsonian and

---

[11] Etienne Gilson, *The Unity of Philosophical Experience* (New York: C. Scribner's Sons, 1937), 306–10, 312–13, 316.

Making Sense of Philosophy

Adlerian ways of making sense of philosophy are far apart. Gilson's way claims to reach doctrinal philosophical conclusions such as the seven just stated. Adler's way achieves at most a dialectical map. Given this situation, there would seem to be little reason not to accept the two as two different ways of approaching and attempting to deal with the great disagreements to be found among the philosophers. Yet that is not the case, at least on one side. As I have already noted, Adler welcomed Gilson's method as applied in *The Unity of Philosophical Experience*. Gilson, on the other hand, refused to see in the Adlerian method any good whatsoever. Why? In seeking an answer to this question, we can learn not only something about the two men, but also about their methods. Since I hold with Adler that both ways lead to much enlightenment, it is Gilson's position that I have difficulty in understanding.

The clearest statement that I know of occurred in a letter that Gilson wrote to me on this subject, dated December 14, 1968, in which he declared:

> I am quite in favor of the Great Books, including the Syntopicon, which is indeed a very great help to philosophical reflection. I do not believe in the Great Ideas, because I do not think that ideas have any real existence outside of definite ideologies, that is, of actual philosophical doctrines in which alone they have existence, growth, and life.... Great Ideas have no more sense by themselves than concepts outside of particular propositions. The mind can proceed from a philosophy to another philosophy, and from an idea as included in a philosophy to a similar one included in another philosophy, but not from a word to the same word in a different philosophical context.

The difficulty that I find in this statement concerns Gilson's understanding of "idea" as he finds it in the use of the Adlerian method. He seems to be equating "idea" with the very word used to express it, as though the word "justice" that appears in the writings, say, of Hume and Rawls, could not possibly mean the same thing. One may admit readily enough that it does not mean exactly the same thing in all the uses of both writers without also denying that there is any common meaning at all. Why then should Gilson want to do so?

The answer, I believe, lies in the crotchet of a historian. In studying the history of philosophical doctrines, Gilson was much interested in the differences and diversities to be found in those doctrines. He was also puzzled by their many disagreements and wanted to offer an explanation of them. From his writings as I know them, his ultimate explanation based the differences upon matters of personal choice and the way that a thinker saw things to be. There is a further complicating factor in the claim that such personal choices and views are incommunicable. I know of no text in which Gilson expressley asserted the incommensurability among basic philosophical positions. However, during my year at Chicago, it was common knowledge among the students of McKeon, himself a student of Gilson, that there were held to be twenty-two basic and incommunicable philosophies. This counts little as evidence, except as the talk among graduate students. However, there is something of a basis for that claim in Gilson's writings.

It appears when he is led to consider why in fact there exist so many different philosophies, and especially Christian philosophies, that all claim to be inspired by

Making Sense of Philosophy

the same Christian faith. Thus in the conclusion of his large book devoted to the thought of Duns Scotus, he asks why Scotus differs so radically in his metaphysics from Saint Thomas. After acknowledging several different subjective factors such as their own talents and education as well as the situation in which they worked, he concludes that when they look at being "they do not see exactly the same thing". The result is that "the only efficacious way in such matters is for each intellect to try to see in its turn that which the other shows while continuing to show itself that which it sees."[12] Such a position regarding basic philosophical differences ultimately reduces to rooting them in personal choices, an option that one takes because that is the way in which things appear to him. Such a position it seems to me, as I am sure that it also does to Adler, is a weak one.

It is weaker still in the view that it takes of ideas. Granted that ideas do not exist by themselves in a Platonic heaven, it does not follow from that that there are no such things as ideas. Indeed, Gilson himself in his search for sense in philosophy was on the trail of ideas. He admits as much in his own writing. His search for the unity of philosophy tells the story of the life of the idea of metaphysics as it attempts to be animated by something other than being, which ends up, he maintains, in metaphysics burying its own undertakers.

Despite Gilson, there is no irreconcilable conflict between his way of making sense of philosophy and Adler's way. If a controversy can be analyzed so as to distinguish

---

[12] Etienne Gilson, *Jean Duns Scot* (Paris: Paris Librairie Philosophique, J. Vrin, 1952), 668.

and identify clearly the basic issues on which disagreement exists, as Adler maintains, it should then be possible for philosophy to pursue its search for a truer answer. Why then cannot the Adlerian way be used as propaedeutic to the kind of doctrinal answer that Gilson sought in his way?

Chapter Six

Recognizing and Holding onto the Center

One of the most illuminating images of the intellectual life is that which concerns a cover. Not that intellectual activity is a cover-up, although at times it may amount to that. It is rather that the intellectual task is to get rid of the cover. Our God is a *Deus absconditus,* and, if hidden, we must seek to find him. For this search we possess three principal methods: Recovering, Discovering, and Uncovering.

As far as these pursuits can be identified with specialized disciplines, they correspond to the activity of history, science, and philosophy. This correspondence, however, at best is only approximate. Historical research in its work of Recovering the past may turn up a find such as that of Schliemann's at the site of Troy that amounts to a Discovery of a reality before thought to be mythical and thus Uncover a whole new dimension of the world portrayed in the epics of Homer, showing that it was not entirely mythical and imaginary.

So too Galileo's Discovery of the craters of the moon and of the moons of Jupiter ended the belief that the observable celestial world differs in matter from that of the earth, a fact that has been confirmed by the astronauts' explorations of the surface of our moon. Hence this Discovery can be claimed as a Recovery of the celestial world for our own terrestrial concerns, thereby also Uncovering the situation such as it had always been without our knowing it.

The task of Uncovering is the most difficult of the three. This fact helps to explain why the work of philosophy, when done as it should be, is more difficult and even less respected than that of history and science. Uncovering demands facing what is already present and taken for granted, as the saying is, but also recognizing that more lies there than meets the eye. To this extent Plato was certainly right in emphasizing the distinction between appearance and reality. The sensible world in which we live and which we experience remains in certain respects the same as it was for Aristotle more than twenty-three hundred years ago, since it remains a world in which change is constantly occurring. Aristotle did not stop the changing. What he did was to note and call attention to the variety of changes occurring before our eyes. Not just change of place, as when we travel from Ann Arbor to Chicago, but also a change in quality as when we come to know a mathematical theorem that we did not know before; or a change in quantity as when we put on weight; or the most radical one of all, the change of generation and corruption as when one comes to be a mortal being and then ceases to be one. All of these are changes, and Aristotle in noting them and calling them to our attention was performing a work of Uncovering. But this work of Aristotle's later led on to the activity of Discovery carried out by the sciences of biology and physics.

These three ways of getting rid of the cover, of penetrating it, have been pursued since they were first Discovered, and at times have had to be Recovered and even Uncovered. At the present age of the world and of our culture, at least in the West, the way of Discovery predominates and enjoys the highest prestige. The way of Uncovering remains the least practiced, the least appreciated. This situation has come about because those who have special responsibility for it, the philosophers, have been wooed away into a kind of research that aims at what can count as Discovery—with, it might be added, very little to show by way of success. Philosophy is not better than it once was, but notoriously worse.

A Work of Recovery

This threefold distinction also provides a way of describing, even of assessing, my own intellectual activities. This present endeavor, insofar as it has consisted in looking back over certain parts of a life, has been a work of Recovery. It has led me to recall and recount what was happening for me, as I now see it, at Ann Arbor, at Chicago, at Toronto, and at Notre Dame, while seeking more or less to make sense of philosophy, as well as to find and hold onto a center.

However in application, the distinction is a slippery one. It works differently for agent and patient, for teacher and student, for writer and subject. What for me in the actual writing of it has been mostly an act of Recovery was for me when it happened and was experienced mostly a work of Discovery. So too the activity of a good teacher may for him involve all three ways of knowing and yet for the student consist mainly in a form of Discovery.

My writing, with but two exceptions, has consisted for the most part in efforts at achieving Recovery. The two exceptions that might count as Discoveries are the dissertation on Del Garbo's commentary on the Cavalcanti poem and the papers that I wrote on the treatise of the Topics in mediaeval logic. Both were the results of original research and produced an addition to present knowledge.

But "research" in the present academic world is a treacherous word. It may provide a convenient excuse for a person to devote his energies to what he considers a higher cause, while actually abandoning the charge that is his main responsibility. Research at the undergraduate level all too frequently amounts to a betrayal by the faculty of the teaching that is owed to the students. I carried out my research into mediaeval logic while primarily engaged in undergraduate teaching. I even offered two courses in the history of logic. But far from being a help to my other undergraduate teaching, these were more of a hindrance. The passion to know is a requisite for a good teacher, but if it is directed solely to a field of research, it proves to be a liability for undergraduate teaching.

As I know from my own experience as well as from observation of academic colleagues, pride is the intellectual temptation of a faculty member, and, along with it, self-centeredness. In the classroom the teacher acts as the captain of the ship that he steers. When he is also teaching the subject of his own research, he runs the additional danger of believing that he is its god and that the subject that he teaches is his and belongs to him as a personal possession.

The only writing that I have done that can count as

one of Uncovering is the work I did for Adler's Institute for Philosophical Research, of which *The Idea of Justice* is the most important. There it was the express aim to lay bare and so Uncover the shape of the underlying controversy concerning justice that was concealed by the many disagreements and counterclaims that covered it.

If biography belongs to history and hence to the pursuit of Recovering, much of the writing that I have done belongs in this division. For in the production of Encyclopaedia Britannica's set of great books, I have written seventy-four of the biographies of the authors included in that set. None of them are long, containing usually between fourteen to fifteen hundred words. None of them can count as a Discovery, since I found nothing new about the lives or the writings that was not already known. Nor by way of interpretation did any pretend to provide new insight into either the life or the work. In fact, these biographical notes were designed to omit anything except information.

I contributed something more in the way of Recovery in the fairly long essays written for *The Great Ideas Today,* the annual volume published for subscribers to the great books set. I have written eight of these, dealing with the works of Euclid, Virgil, Saint Augustine, Saint Thomas, Dante, Cervantes, Montaigne, and Pascal. Each of these essays was written as an introduction to the author's work that appeared in the set, and was meant to enable the reader to gain an entry into the work, to indicate a path that might be followed in the reading of it, and to shed some light along the way.

My most considerable writing at achieving Recovery, which included also some attempt at Uncovering, was the book entitled *Cultures in Conflict: An Essay in the Philosophy of the Humanities.*[1] In it I attempted to describe and analyze the three preeminent intellectual ideals of the Western world: the literary-humanistic ideal of antiquity, the theological ideal of the Middle Ages, and the scientific ideal of the modern world. After this effort at locating and identifying the major contestants, I isolated for analysis four of the major issues on which they were divided, as follows: the quarrel between philosophy and poetry that first became explicit in antiquity, the battle of the seven arts of mediaeval fame, the quarrel of ancients and moderns that came to a head in the seventeenth century, and the two cultures controversy of the 1950s and 1960s. Although each of these issues had a beginning or a high point in a definite historical period, the issues, once they achieved expression, continued to be a focus of discussion and contention. They also brought into discussion other important issues, such as different kinds of language use, feeling and thought, words and ideas, words and things, faith and reason, progress and tradition, and humanities and science. In each case the extreme proponents of one side of an issue tended to dismiss the other as having little weight and hardly deserving discussion. In the analysis of the dispute concerning these issues, I aimed primarily to Uncover and expose the main sources of disagreement. Then after developing a somewhat minimalist theory of the liberal arts and the humanities, I proposed an ecumenical conclusion by placing the blame for intellectual confusion about such matters upon intellectual im-

[1] Otto Bird, *Cultures in Conflict: An Essay in the Philosophy of the Humanities* (Notre Dame, Ind.: Notre Dame University Press, 1976).

perialism. Such imperialism occurs when any one intellectual ideal of what constitutes the best knowledge asserts absolute supremacy and predominance and refuses the right of others to exist or to recognize that other ideals have and can continue to contribute to the intellectual community.

Finding a Center

Uncovering, Recovering, Discovering—any one of these three could not fail to help a person in search of a center to grasp and hold on to. All three I now understand did offer such help to me. As I can recognize now, although I did not at the time, Ann Arbor did in fact establish a beginning for me, and one such as judged by its consequences that confirms T. S. Eliot's lines in the *Four Quartets* that

> What we call the beginning is often the end
> And to make an end is to make a beginning.
> The end is where we start from.[2]

Or as Aristotle put it, the end in view that one would attain is the first principle of action. Thus back beginning in Ann Arbor, I found an end to pursue, one that was founded on a center that I then discovered. Yet at the time that it was happening, I little realized that it was to prove to be a center to which I would hold throughout my life, at least up to this writing, *Deo gratias*.

My reason for going to Ann Arbor to attend the

---

[2] T. S. Eliot, "Little Gidding", in *Four Quartets*, in *The Complete Poems and Plays* (London: Faber and Faber, 1963), 197.

University of Michigan was not responsible, short of the providence of God, for my Discovery. I went to Ann Arbor because I had grown up in the vicinity of the university and because both my uncle and father had graduated from there. My Discovery of the Catholic faith occurred in Ann Arbor, although it also might have happened elsewhere. I do not know about that. I do know that it happened in Ann Arbor, and much that came about thereafter in the other cities was the result of that Discovery. It may well have contributed to developing and increasing my interest in Latin and in the Latin Middle Ages. I believe too that that Discovery must have been largely responsible, in addition to my academic interests, in leading me to Chicago to study Aristotle. Of course, other students were attracted to Chicago for that purpose without having any concern for Catholicism. But I doubt whether I would have gone if I had not also been propelled as a Catholic.

At the University of Chicago the group that I became closely associated with consisted of Catholics, many of them recent converts. This association intensified my interest in Catholic theology and thus became an important reason behind my decision to continue study at the Mediaeval Institute in Toronto, which had been established by the Catholic College of Saint Michael's. There, as I have already related, I intensified my search for the Middle Ages. But more important than gaining skill in that pursuit, I discovered while there a philosophical home in the teaching of Saint Thomas. That Discovery had begun earlier, but it was at Toronto that I learned how the thought of Saint Thomas could be Recovered and thus become available for Uncovering truths about man, nature, and God that lie concealed beneath the appearances of our usual and customary experience. It also followed from my study at the Institute that I went on to teach in Catholic universities, first at Saint John's in Brooklyn, and then at Notre Dame.

I have written much during my professional life. The first writing job by which I earned my living I also owed to the fact that I was a Catholic. It turned out to be my war work for which I was deferred from military service in 1943. I was hired as a philosopher to be turned into a journalist so that I could write for a weekly newsletter published by the Catholic Intercontinental Press. This agency had been established by the Belgian Dominican, Felix A. Morlion, who had fled from Europe to escape the wrath of the Nazis for his anti-Nazi publications in the Low Countries. In New York, with the help of the Americans Frank and Anna Brady, he had obtained help from American government sources to establish a press agency and a weekly organ that aimed to make known the resistance against the Germans of the nascent Christian Democratic parties in Europe. After the end of the war it was these parties that came into power in Western Europe. I wrote for this agency from 1943 to 1947.

The journalistic writing that I did during those few years was scarcely philosophical, even though I was expected to write the "ideological articles" for the weekly newsletter. My writing on the logical topics, on syllogistic, on justice, on the humanities, and on the liberal arts has been philosophical but, with one exception, it has not had any direct bearing upon the thought and teaching of Saint Thomas. Indeed, much of my reading, teaching, and writing has been directed to the great books. Why then should I claim that it is my belief in and practice of the Catholic faith that was the center for me and my work, and not the great books? My answer to that question has already been given. The great books of the Western tradition, as represented in the set published by Encyclopaedia Britannica, Inc., may make a sceptic or an eclectic in philosophy, but nothing else. I was protected from that eventuality from the beginning of my close association with them by my devotion to Saint Thomas. Furthermore, in recent years my writing upon those books has been confined for the most part to those by Catholic authors.

However, my work in both teaching and writing has not always dealt with subjects or themes expressly Catholic or religious, except for the instances I have already mentioned. Gilson once wrote an essay on the subject of "The Intelligence in the Service of Christ the King",[3] and at least in intention, inspiration, and hope, that too has been my aim. For such a service to succeed at least two requirements have to be met. As a work of intelligence it requires a mastery of the techniques of the intelligence, and as a service of Christ who is known as King and Lord by faith, it requires the techniques of supernatural theology. And now for more than fifty years I have been endeavoring, as I still am, to acquire and perfect my abilities in those two techniques.

---

[3] Etienne Gilson, "The Intelligence in the Service of Christ the King," in *A Gilson Reader,* ed. A. C. Pegis (Garden City, N.Y.: Doubleday & Co, 1957), 31–48.

Curriculum Vitae

1914	Born July 3, Ann Arbor, Michigan, son of Walter Duane Bird and Mary Snyder Bird
1916	Divorce of parents
1920–24	Public elementary school in Ann Arbor
1924–27	Public elementary school in Detroit, Michigan
1927	June 3, death of mother
1927–28	University high school in Ann Arbor
1928–31	Public high school in Nogales, Arizona
1931–36	University of Michigan, Ann Arbor, Michigan
1935	A.B. degree, Honors in English
1936	M.A. degree, English and Comparative Literature
1936	October 31, married Evelina Bills Polk, resulting in eight children
1936–37	University of Chicago, in graduate philosophy
1937–39	University of Toronto, Pontifical Institute of Mediaeval Studies
1938–39	Teaching Fellow in Philosophy, St. Michael's College
1939	Ph.D. in Philosophy, University of Toronto

1939–43	Assistant Professor of Philosophy, St. John's University, Brooklyn, N.Y.
1943–46	Associate Editor, *CIP Correspondence,* a weekly newsletter published in New York City by the Catholic Intercontinental Press
1946–50	Associate Editor of the *Syntopicon,* the analytical index of *Great Books of the Western World,* published by Encyclopaedia Britannica, Inc.
1950–63	Associate Professor, Founder, and 1st Director of the General Program of Liberal Studies, University of Notre Dame
1952–	Fellow of the Institute for Philosophical Research
1964–70	Executive Editor of *The Great Ideas Today,* the annual volume for subscribers to *Great Books of the Western World*
1970	University Professor of Arts and Letters, Notre Dame
1973–74	Fellow, Ecumenical Institute, Saint John's College, Minnesota
1977	Retired from Notre Dame as Professor Emeritus
1977–87	Established vineyard in Martin County, Indiana
1986	Distinguished Professor of Philosophy, University of Dallas

Publications

(excluding book reviews)

"The Canzone d'Amore of Cavalcanti According to the Commentary of Dino del Garbo". *Mediaeval Studies* 2 (1940): 150–203; (1941), 117–60.

In *Great Books of the Western World* (Chicago: Encyclopaedia Britannica, 1952), the following biographical notes:

Plato
Aristotle
Plotinus
Augustine
Aquinas
Machiavelli
Descartes

Hobbes
Berkeley
Montesquieu
Rousseau
The Federalists
J. S. Mill

"How to Read an Article of the *Summa*". *The New Scholasticism* 28, no. 2 (April 1953): 129–59.

"Dialectic in Philosophical Inquiry". *Dialectica* 9, no. 3/4 (1955): 287–304.

"Science and Mathematics in the Liberal Arts Curriculum". *The Journal of General Education* 10, no. 1 (January 1957): 24–29.

"The Logical Interest of the Topics as Seen in Abelard". *The Modern Schoolman* (November 1959): 53–57.

"Peirce's Theory of Methodology". *Philosophy of Science* 26, no. 3 (July 1959): 187–200.

"The Formalizing of the Topics in Mediaeval Logic". *Notre Dame Journal of Formal Logic* 1, no. 4 (1960): 138–49.

"The Re-discovery of the Topics". *Mind* 70, N.S., no. 280 (October 1961): 534–39.

"Topic and Consequence in Ockham's Logic". *Notre Dame Journal of Formal Logic* 2, no. 2 (1961): 65–78.

"The Tradition of the Logical Topics: Aristotle to Ockham". *Journal of the History of Ideas* 23, no. 3 (July-September 1962): 307–23.

"What Peirce Means by Leading Principles". *Notre Dame Journal of Formal Logic* 3, no. 3 (July 1962): 175–78.

In *Gateway to the Great Books* (Chicago: Encyclopaedia Britannica, 1963), the following introductions to:

Grotius: "Prolegomena to the Law of War and Peace"
Voltaire: "English Men and Ideas"
Epictetus: "The Enchiridion"
Epicurus: "Letters to Herodotus and Menoeceus"
James: "The Will to Believe; The Sentiment of Rationality"
Pascal: "The Art of Persuasion"
Mill: "Nature"
Voltaire: "The Philosophy of Common Sense"

"The History of Logic". *Review of Metaphysics* 16, no. 3 (March 1963): 491–502.

"The Complexity of Love". *Thought* (Summer 1964): 210–20.

Syllogistic and Its Extensions, Englewood Cliffs, N.J.: Prentice-Hall, 1964.

"Wealth and Happiness in Great Books of the Western World". In *The Great Ideas Today, 1965*. Chicago: Encyclopedia Britannica, 1965, 90–96.

"Work and Leisure in Great Books of the Western World, In *The Great Ideas Today, 1965*. Chicago: Encyclopaedia Britannica, 1965, 97–104.

"Woman in Great Books of the Western World". In *The Great Ideas Today, 1966*, 72–81. Chicago: Encyclopaedia Britannica, 1966.

The Idea of Justice, New York: Praeger, 1967.

"The Idea of Religion in Great Books of the Western World". In *The Great Ideas Today, 1967*, 70–80. Chicago: Encyclopaedia Britannica, 1967.

"The Idea of Equality". In *The Great Ideas Today, 1968*, 303–50. Chicago: Encyclopaedia Britannica, 1968.

"Veatch on the Humanities". *The New Scholasticism* 44, no. 1 (April 1970): 125–32.

With Thomas J. Musial, "Great Books Programs". In *Encyclopaedia of Library and Information Service*, vol. 10, 159–79. New York: Marcel Dekker, 1973.

In *Encyclopaedia Britannica*, 15th ed. (Chicago: Encyclopaedia Britannica, 1974), the following entries:

Bergson, Henri	Kant, Immanuel
Humanities	Lesniewski, Stanislaw

"The Idea of Justice". In *The Great Ideas Today, 1974*, 166–205. Chicago: Encyclopaedia Britannica, 1974.

"The Relevance of Philosophy Today". In 1975 Britannica Book of the Year. Chicago: Encyclopaedia Britannica, 1975.

Cultures in Conflict: An Essay in the Philosophy of the Humanities. Notre Dame, Ind.: University of Notre Dame Press, 1976.

"In Memoriam Ivo Thomas (1912–1976)". *Notre Dame Journal of Formal Logic* 18, no. 2 (April 1977): 193–94.

"The Topics and the Art of Teaching by Discussion". In *Paideia,* Special Aristotle Issue (1978): 196–201.

"Ethics in a Permissive Society: The Controversy Regarding the Objectivity of Moral Values". In *The Great Ideas Today, 1981,* 160–86. Chicago: Encyclopaedia Britannica, 1981.

"Rethinking the *Pensées* of Pascal". In *The Great Ideas Today, 1982,* 212–36. Chicago: Encyclopaedia Britannica, 1983.

"Dante the Thinker: Poetry and Philosophy". In *The Great Ideas Today, 1983,* 204–35. Chicago: Encyclopaedia Britannica, 1983.

"The Ambiguities of Don Quixote". In *The Great Ideas Today, 1984,* 94–122. Chicago: Encyclopaedia Britannica, 1984.

"The Christian Skepticism of Montaigne". In *The Great Ideas Today, 1985,* 120–49. Chicago: Encyclopaedia Britannica, 1985.

"On Reading Euclid". In *The Great Ideas Today, 1986,* 184–216. Chicago: Encyclopaedia Britannica, 1986.

"On Reading the *Summa:* An Introduction to St. Thomas Aquinas". In *The Great Ideas Today, 1987,* 126–54. Chicago: Encyclopaedia Britannica, 1987.

"St. Augustine on Reading". In *The Great Ideas Today, 1988*, 132–61. Chicago: Encyclopaedia Britannica, 1988.

"A Dialectical Version of Philosophical Discussion". In *Freedom in the Modern World*. Edited by M. D. Torre. 57–64. Notre Dame, Ind.: American Maritain Association, 1989.

"Virgil and Hippocrites: A Reading of the Georgics". In *The Great Ideas Today, 1989*, 103–22. Chicago: Encyclopaedia Britannica, 1989.

"Great Books and Liberal Arts". In *The Great Ideas of Today, 1991*. Chicago: Encyclopaedia Britannica, 1991.

Biographies written for *Great Books of the Western World* (Chicago: Encyclopaedia Britannica), in 1988–89:

1. Austen, Jane
2. Balzac
3. Barth, Karl
4. Beckett
5. Bergson
6. Bohr
7. Born
8. Brecht
9. Calvin
10. Cather
11. Chekhov
12. Conrad
13. Dewey
14. Dickens
15. Dobzhansky
16. Eddington
17. Einstein
18. Eliot, George
19. Eliot, T. S.
20. Frazer
21. Erasmus
22. Faulkner
23. Fitzgerald, F. S.
24. Hardy
25. Heidegger
26. Heisenberg
27. Hemingway
28. Huizinga
29. Ibsen
30. James, Henry
31. James, William
32. Joyce

33. Kafka
34. Keynes
35. Kierkegaard
36. Lawrence
37. Levi-Strauss
38. Malinowski
39. Mann
40. Molière
41. Nietzsche
42. O'Neill
43. Orwell
44. Pirandello
45. Planck
46. Poincaré
47. Proust
48. Racine
49. Russell
50. Schrödinger
51. Shaw
52. Tawney
53. Tocqueville
54. Twain
55. Veblen
56. Voltaire
57. Waddington
58. Weber
59. Whitehead
60. Wittgenstein
61. Woolf

Index of Persons

Adler, Mortimer: association of Otto Bird with, 11, 44–45; on controversy in philosophy, 115–16; on Gilson's philosophy, 105, 119, 121; and Great Books, 73–80; and Institute for Philosophical Research, 127; philosophy of, 101, 106–8, 114, 115–22; as professor, 42, 46–49, 50; and Saint Thomas Aquinas, 43; and *Syntopicon,* 73–75, 76; and University of Chicago, 37–39; and University of Notre Dame, 77, 78, 79
Anselm, Saint, 103
Apollonius, 76
Archimedes, 76
Apostle, Hippocrates, 42
Aquinas, Saint Thomas. *See* Thomas Aquinas, Saint
Aristotle: and dialectic, 110, 116–17; in history of philosophy, 83, 99, 100; influence of on Saint Thomas Aquinas, 67–68, 71; on knowledge, 85–86; on love, 24–27, 29; on moving toward the final end, 72, 129; philosophy of, 62, 114, 124
Ashley, O. P., Winston, 44
Auden, W. H., 19
Augustine, Saint: doctrinal traits of, 102–4; in history of philosophy, 83, 99; and love, 26, 72; on the Platonists, 57–59; philosophy of, 65, 69–70; and Ro-

man history, 71; as teacher, 67, 68

Barr, Stringfellow, 39, 40
Barrett, William, 42
Beeson, Charles H., 51
Berkeley, George, 100
Bird, Evelina Bills Polk, wife of Otto, 133
Bird, Mary Snyder, mother of Otto, 32, 35, 133
Bird, Walter Duane, father of Otto, 15, 32, 35, 133
Bird, Calla N., grandmother of Otto, 14–15
Bird, Jean E., sister of Otto, 32
Bloch, Marc, 54
Bochenski, I. M., 62
Boethius, Anicius Manlius Severinus, 62
Bolt, Robert, 9
Bonaventure, Saint, 65, 103
Brady, Anna, 131
Brady, Frank, 131
Brennan, C. S. C., Father Thomas J., 78–79
Buchanan, Scott: and Great Books, 40, 76; as professor, 46, 48–50; and University of Chicago, 39, 42

Carnap, Rudolf, 41
Cavalcanti, Guido, 23, 59–61
Cavanaugh, C. S. C., Father John J., 45, 77–80, 97
Cervantes Saavedra, Miguel de, 16
Chesterton, Gilbert Keith, 9, 15, 21
Cicero, Marcus Tullius, 26
Comte, Auguste, 118
Copernicus, Nicolaus, 76
Crowe, Michael, 95

Dante Alighieri, 23, 83
D'Arcy, M. C., 27
de Brabant, Siger, 64
De Wulf, Maurice, 65
del Garbo, Dino, 23, 60–61
Del Vecchio, Giorgio, 112
Denomy, C. S. B., Father Alexandre, 56
Descartes, René: and Augustine, 104; on controversy in philosophy, 115; in history of

philosophy, 99, 100, 106; and metaphysics, 118
Dewey, John, 38, 41
Dryden, John, 84
Duns Scotus, John, 121

Eliot, T. S., 30, 31, 59, 83, 129
Erskine, John, 73, 80
Euclid, 75

Febvre, Lucien, 54
Foster, Kenelm, 68
Freud, Sigmund, 26, 76

Galileo Galilei, 76, 123
Gilson, Étienne: 9, 132; on Adler's philosophy, 107, 119–20; and "Aeterni Patris", 65, 66; on Augustine, 57, 59, 102–3; on Duns Scotus, 121; and the Institute of Mediaeval Studies, 51–55; philosophy of, 83, 101–6, 117–22; on Pound's review, 59–60; as professor, 49, 56–57, 80; on Saint Thomas Aquinas, 64, 121
Goodman, Paul, 42

Gorman, William, 42, 74
Gui, Bernard, 68

Hans, Otto, uncle of Otto Bird, 13, 32–33
Hazo, Robert G., 23, 108
Hegel, George Wilhelm Friedrich, 100, 112, 116
Heidegger, Martin, 69, 100
Hesburgh, C. S. C., Father Theodore, 93, 95
Hobbes, Thomas, 114
Homer, 83, 123
Hopwood, Avery, 30
Hume, David, 100, 114, 120
Hutchins, Robert Maynard: and Great Books, 74, 78, 82; and *Syntopicon,* 76; and University of Chicago, 37–39, 43

James, William, 20, 38, 41
Job, 71
Joyce, James, 83
Justin Martyr, Saint, 65

Kant, Immanuel, 99, 100, 107, 115, 118
Kepler, Johannes, 76
Kiley, Roger J., 78

LaDrière, Craig, 45
Leibniz, Gottfried Wilhelm, 63, 69
Leo XIII, Pope, 64–66
Lewis, C. S., 27, 29
Locke, John, 100

Malebranche, Nicolas de, 103
Manion, Dean Clarence, 78
Maritain, Jacques, 53, 56, 83
Marx, Karl, 76, 116
McGill, V. J., 108
McInerny, Ralph, 9–11
McKeon, Richard P.: and Gilson, 120; as grammarian, 46, 48–49; as professor, 41, 43, 48, 50; and University of Chicago, 39
Mead, George Herbert, 38
Mill, John Stuart, 114
Milton, John, 31, 83
More, Saint Thomas. *See* Thomas More, Saint
Morlion, O. P., Felix A., 131
Muckle, C. S. B., Father Joseph T., 56

Newman, John Henry Cardinal, 16–18, 92
Newton, Isaac, 76, 99
Nicomachus, 76
Noel, Leon, 65
Nutting, Willis, 78
Nygren, Anders, 27

Oesterle, Jean, 44
Oesterle, John, 44
O'Malley, Frank, 78
Ormsby, John, 20

Paul, Saint, 67
Pegis, Anton, 80–81, 86
Peirce, C. S., 41
Phelan, Father Gerald B., 56, 65
Plato, 82; on appearance and reality, 124; and dialectic, 116; in history of philosophy, 83, 99, 100; influence of on Saint Thomas Aquinas, 67
Plotinus, 57–59, 67, 83, 100
Pound, Ezra, 30, 59–60, 83
Ptolemy, 76

Quixote, Don, 18–20

Ranke, Leopold von, 81
Ratner, Herbert, 44
Rauch, Rufus, 78
Rawls, John, 115, 120
Reinhard, John, 22, 46
Rich, Richard, 9
Ross, Alf, 114
Russell, Bertrand, 42, 63

Sancho, 19
Scheler, Max, 26
Schliemann, Heinrich, 123
Schwartz, Herbert, 42–43, 44, 46–47
Shaw, J. E., 60–61
Shook, C. S. B., Father Laurence K., 52, 54, 65, 107
Siguenza, Jose de, 6
Simon, Kenneth "Bud," 43
Sparks, O. P., Father Timothy, 43
Stern, Margaret, 44
Stump, Eleonore, 63–64

Thèry, Pére G., 55
Thomas Aquinas, Saint: on faith, 93; influence of on Otto Bird, 73, 130, 131–32; as intellectual foundation, 64, 66, 87, 98; on love, 26, 72; and philosophy, 83, 99; Pope Leo XIII on, 64, 65; teaching of, 66–73, 121; and University of Chicago, 43; writing style of, 48
Thomas, Ivo, 62
Thomas More, Saint, 9
Torre, M. D., 106
Tufts, James, 38

Van Doren, Charles, 108
Virgil, 83, 84

Wallis, Charles Glenn, 40
Whitehead, Alfred North, 63
Wilbur, Richard, 10
Wittgenstein, Ludwig, 99, 100, 115

Yeats, W. B., 6, 16

Zucker, Alice, 44

B 945 .B48 A3 1991
Bird, Otto A., 1914-
Seeking a center